*Praise for Janelle Lynnae's*
## FLEX YOUR CONFIDENCE MUSCLE

"Janelle is here to help you SOAR! She leads with heart, authenticity & is truly passionate about showing you the tangible actions you can take—NOW—to make huge leaps forward in your career. Run, don't walk, to check out her new book!"

**MEGGIE PALMER**
Founder of the PepTalkHer App

"If you're looking for motivation, inspiration, and actionable tips to boost your confidence—this is it! So many amazing takeaways—ranging from concrete steps on how to level up to deep life insights."

**OLIVIA**
Next Level Confident Community Member

"Janelle makes confidence fun and tangible with her humor and genuine desire to help others. If you've ever felt stuck about reaching the next level in life—be it in your career, relationship or health—*Flex Your Confidence Muscle* is here to show you how to break through your mental barriers and create the life you've dreamed of!"

**GEN COHEN**
CEO of Gen's Gym

"If you are looking to find content that will challenge you to be the best version of yourself, look no further. This will inspire you to rewire your mindset and encourage you to be great!"

Next Level Confident Community Member

"Janelle brings so much energy and passion with just the right amount of empathy to meet you where you are to challenge, elevate and empower you to be the best version of yourself. If you are looking for an impactful step-by-step guide that translates into measurable results, her new book is a must have!"

**WENDY MERCHANT**
Founder and Executive Director at STEMblazers

"If you're someone who has ever struggled with self-doubt, self-sabotage, or lack of confidence and it's prevented you from going after what you truly want in life, let Janelle lead the way. Janelle is genuine and honest while giving you a no BS approach on how you can actually take control and change your life."

**CLAIRE GUENTZ**
Content Creator & Founder of the Parry App

"Janelle is a force to be reckoned with. She keeps it fun while also tackling uncomfortable, real, worthwhile topics. I always leave feeling empowered to be better than before!"

**LAURA**
Next Level Confident Community Member

"This has helped me soooo much in my journey to discover who I want to be and what I believe my purpose in life is! Struggling with both depression and anxiety hasn't been easy at all; but Janelle encourages me to continue and push forward!"

Next Level Confident Community Member

"Janelle is passionate about helping women build their confidence muscle! Her actionable tools are invaluable in supporting the advancement of women in their careers,"

**CYRONNE COUNTS**
Women In Product Director of Programs

"Janelle is open and authentic, creating a safe space. It's refreshing to learn that even smart, accomplished women all experience similar feelings and challenges related to our confidence. The biggest takeaway for me has been learning to reflect on and own my truths which has changed my perspective both personally and professionally. I have a renewed sense of direction and confidence that I can achieve the previously elusive "what's next" in my career and personal life."

**KAREN RICE**
The WICT Network Rocky Mountain Director of General Programming

"This girl is the real deal. She shows vulnerability and transparency when it comes to herself and her relationships. If you're looking for content that puts a smile on your face and gets you thinking... this is it!"

Next Level Confident Community Member

# FLEX YOUR
## *Confidence*
# MUSCLE

# JANELLE LYNNAE

# FLEX YOUR
## *Confidence*
# MUSCLE

**HOW TO OVERCOME YOUR LIMITING BELIEFS
AND FINALLY TAKE ACTION**

# FLEX YOUR CONFIDENCE MUSCLE

## HOW TO OVERCOME YOUR LIMITING BELIEFS AND FINALLY TAKE ACTION

### JANELLE LYNNAE

Published and distributed by Merack Publishing

Library of Congress Control Number: 2022909779

ISBN Paperback 978-1-957048-48-2
Hardcover 978-1-957048-50-5
eBook 978-1-957048-49-9

# DEDICATION

For my husband & best friend, Frankie.

For my loving parents, Jeff & Melody.

And for you, the reader. You are why I wrote this book.

# CONTENTS

# INTRODUCTION

You will never feel 100% ready to make a change. If you are waiting for the "right moment" when your confidence is at an all-time high, every area of your life is going just perfectly, you're making great money, your time management is on point, and all your relationships are going smoothly—it's never going to happen.

One of the top limiting beliefs I wrestle with is that I'm just not QUITE ready yet. That I need to be just a liiiiitttle bit "further along" before I can get started on that really audacious thing. It is actually a hilarious oxymoron when you think about it. The longer I wait, the more time passes by, and I'm still feeling unqualified because I still haven't done the audacious thing that would "qualify" me. I don't know about you, but I'm DONE waiting for the "right time" to get started!

This book is about how I went from the girl who stayed small because of my limiting beliefs, to the woman I am today who believes so fully in my worth and is proudly and confidently taking up space.

My hope in writing this book for you is that you are able to have that same transformation. My deepest desire is that you will have relentless, unwavering confidence in who you are, exactly as you are today. That your confidence isn't just a cute mantra on a t-shirt or a beautifully written post on Instagram, but instead it's your unshakably high self-worth that strengthens you to move mountains.

And my hope for this book is that it will help you on your journey to finding this deep-rooted confidence. That by reading my extremely vulnerable, unedited story and my most debilitating limiting beliefs, you will become aware of the limiting beliefs you are subconsciously buying into daily.

This book will not only help you uncover your own limiting beliefs but, more importantly, will start the journey of freeing you from those lies. This book is meant to empower you by showing you the truth so you can begin believing the truth. With your new thought patterns in place, you will be able to take committed action on your most audacious ideas and start living a life that you're truly proud of.

I'm going to help you reflect on your own story and remember parts of your past that formed you into the woman you are today. With this powerful reflection, you'll be able to forgive and heal from your past and begin to write a new story from a place of resolute truth. I want you to believe beyond a shadow of doubt that your life matters and that you were born with a purpose.

I want you to punch your limiting beliefs in the face, so you can stop playing small and can finally expand into living the badass life you were meant to. After you conquer these limiting beliefs, you'll be able to more easily grow into your absolute fullest potential. You'll become powerful. Unstoppable. Limitless.

> Your life matters and you can do whatever you put your mind to. It's time to flex your confidence muscle.

As you read on, you'll learn that writing this book was not easy for me. In fact, I spent years telling myself all the reasons why I couldn't do it. I didn't think I was ready yet. I heard the whisper calling me to share my story so I could help women break free from their lies, but I kept putting it off until the timing was right. I ignored the whisper right up until the moment God essentially threw a cold glass of water into my face and I couldn't deny this calling any longer.

I needed to throw out my limiting beliefs and focus on why I was the right person to share this message with you.

Honestly, the main reason I DO actually feel qualified to write this book is BECAUSE of my own journey and struggle. While I'm still sooo far from perfect, I have been able to powerfully shift my mindset from negative thought patterns to empowered thought patterns and I've seen the insanely amazing results that come from finally believing in myself.

Maybe, like me, you have an angel on one shoulder and a devil on the other. The angel says you can do whatever you put your mind to. And the devil tells you how much you suck, that you're not good enough or special enough. I have retrained my brain to be able to step into this place where I believe that I'm worthy. I realized that I don't have to be perfect in order to teach someone how to do something. I keep taking risky, messy actions over and over again! I can share what I've learned and what I know, and still make mistakes along the way.

It's incredible that I get to speak for Fortune 500 companies and that I've gotten to teach thousands of women how to build confidence in the workplace using their mindset! It's amazing that I get to use my social media platforms to give practical tools for self-growth to my badass audience. It blows my mind that I've gotten the privilege of coaching hundreds of women individually on how to shift their thought patterns in order to begin attracting new results. I'm truly so grateful for all of these beautiful opportunities.

In every venue or platform, my message is essentially the same. I want to share with you the number one foundational idea that shifted my own mindset. Learning and accepting this simple truth has changed everything: My beliefs lead to my thoughts, my thoughts lead to my actions and my actions lead to my results.

For the longest time I didn't have the results I wanted in most areas of my life. I wasn't happy in my romantic relationships or my career path. I didn't really think my life mattered. So I accepted the mediocrity. When I learned about the power of my mind, it was a huge shift because I realized I get to LITERALLY choose my own reality. Boom! Mind blown.

Everything started to change around me. I broke up with my boyfriend of six years and I moved to California by myself without a job. I drastically shifted my career path and I changed my finances. I started taking action on my life because I finally realized that my life *actually* mattered. I gave myself permission to dream big. The result is that I'm now living the magical life I've always wanted to. I have to pinch myself sometimes because it's hard to believe this is my reality. For so long I felt incredibly undeserving of a life like this.

I'm an entrepreneur. I run my own business—it's pretty dang successful if I do say so myself—and I believe I'm fulfilling my purpose. I married the man of my dreams, he's my absolute best friend. I live in the most beautiful city in the entire world and get to walk by the ocean every day. And I'm genuinely happy, grateful and peaceful at least 97% of the time!

There are obviously still new levels for me to reach and limiting beliefs for me to overcome. **For every new level, there's a new devil.** It's a constant process of overcoming. I know that anything I don't have right now is because of a shift that gets to happen in my mindset. (Notice I said "gets" and not "needs." I always replace the word "need" with "get," as it's a powerful word shift.)

This is the story I want to share with you: How I went from the girl who spent years suffering the consequences of my victim mentality, my fixed, scarcity mindset, to the beautifully imperfect person I am today that has an empowered, growth, and abundance mindset and who has faith in the expansive possibilities in store for my life. While I still battle against some limiting beliefs, I've broken through a lot of my barriers and have seen the glorious potential that exists on the other side. I hope that by sharing my experience, I can help you uncover your own limiting beliefs, and create new, empowered thought patterns to finally start taking action on your audacious goals and dreams! And when it comes to flexing your confidence muscle, *that* is the ultimate flex.

*Part One*

# LAYING THE
# FOUNDATION

*Chapter 1*

# SILENCING MY SELF-SABOTAGE

It would be easier on my ego if I only chose to share the limiting beliefs I've already overcome so I could impress you with my awesomeness. I've noticed that's what a lot of leaders do because it's much less vulnerable that way. But the truth is, I still have a lot of limiting beliefs to work through. Let's talk about how unqualified I felt to write this book, for starters.

It was mid-August 2021, around 6:45am, when I was finishing up my typical morning journaling routine, enjoying a quiet fifteen minutes on the couch before Frankie, my husband, would be coming home from his early morning workout. I couldn't tell you what I read that day and also have no idea what I wrote down as the three things I was grateful for in my journal. I'm pretty sure my candles were lit and that the smell was a mix of musky and sweet (which has always been my favorite smell for both candles and perfumes).

The one detail I remember clearly is this: I was putting my journal, Bible and prayer book back inside of my favorite West Elm coffee table, when I heard a soft whisper that said, "What if you started writing your book today?"

I had been toying around with the idea of writing a book for a year or two at that point, and it definitely wasn't the first time I had heard that whisper, though those gut-feeling type whispers seemed to be happening more and more. That August morning, I did what I always did when I started thinking about my book—I disqualified myself.

I dismissed the idea for a thousand reasons. For starters, I had no reason to write a book in that season of my life. If anything, my life felt like it was unraveling and I barely knew what direction my business was headed in. Truthfully, I felt more lost about my career path than I'd felt in years.

I had spent the last three and a half years building a business (Next Level Confident) that never FELT fully successful. (At least financially, because my business wasn't making a million dollars annually. In my mind, that felt like the real measure of success, which might sound ridiculous to some of you, I know.) In the last six months I kept hearing the whisper to let my business go. But I didn't want to let it go. I wanted to make it work. Next Level Confident was, and is, my baby.

I wanted to build it into the business I had been dreaming of since I started my journey as an entrepreneur. I was mad at myself for not being able to scale it the way I wanted to. And not being able to figure it out was infuriating! I always figure things out. If I let go of my business, what would I do? This is all I had. I had put all my eggs in this basket.

That morning, hearing the book whisper yet again, my mind swirled with these objections and limiting beliefs:

**Objection A:** My audience is too small, and no one would read the book. I would pour my heart and soul into it and then it would sell approximately seven copies. Even the people who bought it wouldn't read it. It would just be a nice gesture that my parents and a few close friends would make out of sympathy.

**Objection B:** This book would never make me any money (obviously, because only seven people would buy it) so I would make liiiiike… twenty dollars in profit maybe? Given that it would likely take me approximately eighty hours to write, I would make twenty-five cents an hour, which feels like an inefficient use of my time… again, obviously. (Also, the joke is on me, because this book actually took WAY more than eighty hours to write!)

**Objection C:** Maybe I'm just writing this book to feed my selfish, greedy ego. Every public speaker writes a book. You can brag about it to your fans, clients, friends and family so they think you're actually so much cooler than you are. In fact, every article on how to become a public speaker tells you to write a book so that you can charge more when you speak. What if the only reason I want to write a book is because I'm actually extremely selfish and don't care if anyone reads it? I'm just doing it to look impressive and make more money when I speak?

**Objection D:** I already tried writing an ebook. In fact, I'd tried not once but TWICE! And you know what? I sold less than ten copies of each over the course of a year!! I mean if that's not failure then I don't know what is!

Okay bear with me, I have another objection as to why writing a book right now is the worst timing ever:

**Objection E:** There are thousands of people writing books. Some are great, some are horrible. But I am just me. I don't have the qualifications of having one hundred thousand Instagram followers (yet) or making millions of dollars per year. So, who am I to write a book, ya know?

But despite all of these limiting beliefs screaming in my head, I could still hear the whisper pushing me to write a book.

I remember the exact moment I was able to envision this book with perfect clarity. I was popping my pimples before bed (like I always promise myself I'll stop doing one of these days) and while popping away, I started randomly thinking of book title ideas. What if I called my book *Punch Your Limiting Beliefs in the Face*? I laughed to myself and decided to make a note of the book idea to use some day down the road (far far down the road, in a few years, when the time was right!)

A few weeks later, I was headed to Miami for one of my very best friend's bachelorette parties. I landed Friday at quarter to six in the evening and was ready for an incredible weekend with the gals! The bride wanted to include her mom and mother-in-law in the celebrations, so on Saturday morning we took a break from our "wild" bachelorette activities to host an elegant bridal shower. It was there, on this sunny, humid, Florida morning, that something strange happened. One of the women (who I literally had JUST met for the first time in my entire life the night prior) looked into my eyes during lunch and said, "God gave me a word for you: you're supposed to write a book. Have you ever thought about writing a book?"

I instantly started crying—like, ugly crying—in the middle of this fancy bridal shower and yes, it was definitely awkward.

> But sometimes these awkward moments are the ones that provide our biggest breakthroughs in life.

At that moment, it didn't feel like a breakthrough, though. It felt like a major inconvenience. My thoughts were racing, "Why is she saying this?? Ugh! Noo! I can't do this. Make it go away!" The thought made me feel so inadequate and sick to my stomach.

As I flew home from the bachelorette party Monday afternoon, I began thinking about all of the times I had heard the whisper over the past few months and how everything inside of me kept saying, "Thanks, but I don't want to. Maybe later." I kept thinking about that woman's comment at the shower because it felt like God finally grew so impatient with me ignoring the whispers that he sent a message to me in human form.

On the plane ride home, I heard another whisper. It said, "Do you trust me?" It sounded like God. Shoulder to shoulder with complete strangers, I found myself having another awkward and unwelcome crying moment.

I began to pray.

Now, I know not everyone reading this book believes in God or prayer, but stick with me, because I'm sure we've all begged for a "sign" once or twice…

*God, I know I'm supposed to say yes to trusting you but, damn, I really don't know if I can trust you on this one. Also I'm not sure that it's even you that keeps nudging this. Maybe it's just me being selfish or impulsive or crazy. If this is really you, can you please confirm it one more time this week? Or… I don't know… maybe I've had enough confirmation already but I just keep resisting it no matter how many confirmations I get. How am I supposed to know? God, why now? What would I even write about? Who would read my story? What would be the purpose of the book? Are you going to bless it like crazy, God? Or is this just a test and I'm supposed to do it even if it flops?*

The whisper asked again, "Do you trust me, no matter what?"

I am a firm believer that God works all things out for good. So at that moment, I responded, "Yes. I will trust you."

If He was asking me to do this then there had to be a reason why. I realized in that moment I had been rebelling against something that God had in store for me and that this calling wasn't even about me. I chose trust.

God was saying, "Stop worrying about *you* and start thinking about other people."

Ouch. That hurt to hear.

Maybe it was actually selfish *not* to write the book…

I finally understood that my calling in this season is to serve other women who read this story. My job is simply to have faith that my words might change their lives. It doesn't matter how many copies of the book I sell or how "successful" it's going to be. I realized that by waiting until I was "perfectly qualified" to write the "perfect book," I was holding back valuable messages that could really make a difference in a woman's life. By taking action, and also facing my own current limiting beliefs, I was being selfless.

I basically just needed to get out of my own way.

*Chapter 2*

# THE POWER OF REFLECTION

Just like many of the women I've spoken to and coached, and maybe like some of you, I used to struggle with feeling like I "didn't belong" or the other people were "further along" and smarter than me. I had constant imposter syndrome in a room full of people that I deemed more successful than me and smarter than me. And when I did speak up, I would replay everything I said later, over-analyzing my words, ruminating for hours, wishing I could have said it better, wondering if everyone thought I was dumb.

Then, through reading books, listening to podcasts, attending conferences and hiring coaches, I became aware of something the personal development world talks about a lot: limiting beliefs. I realized the stories of not belonging and not mattering and not being cool enough were just that—stories.

Now, I've retrained my brain and I've learned how to step into my power. Now, I believe I belong in a room full of smart, talented, powerful people. Now, I believe that I'm capable of doing anything I put my mind to. Now, I've changed my story. I am smart enough. I am worthy and loveable, just as I am today. I realized I can be a badass with my mess and imperfections too.

And that's why I wrote this book for you. Because women like us are FAR too hard on ourselves. It's time for you to intentionally rewrite your stories and step into your power. It's time to learn the tools to flex your confidence muscle, see yourself as the valuable badass that you are—even on the days when you aren't perfect, even on the days when you fall flat on your face and want to curl up in a ball and cry it out.

Your awesomeness doesn't depend on you having a specific job title or relationship status or amount of money in the bank. Your awesomeness is innately set inside of you. Nothing and no one can take it away, except you. You get to choose how you perceive yourself despite external circumstances that, at times, might try to tell you otherwise.

Let's talk about why we doubt our own badassery and how our beliefs have a ripple effect on everything in life.

**Beliefs ⟶ Thoughts ⟶ Actions ⟶ Results**

I mentioned this powerful statement in the intro. I shared how learning and accepting this simple truth changed everything for me. If you keep believing the same thing, then your result will never change. In order to get a new result for your life, you get to change what you believe is possible for you.

Let's say, for example, you were raised in a household where you were told subliminally that a man's opinion matters more than a woman's opinion. That men are supposed to chase their career and women are supposed to chase men. That women are made for the kitchen and for providing babies. And that women are supposed to be nice, sweet, kind, and agreeable.

If you have those limiting beliefs unknowingly floating around in the back of your mind, you might be struggling at work. Maybe you're not making the amount of money you want to be making, and maybe you feel guilty for loving your career so much. Maybe you find yourself biting your tongue in important meetings. Especially when it's a room filled with more senior men, and you never seem to have the courage to speak up to share your opinion. That is the RESULT of a belief pattern that you haven't become aware of or, if you are aware of it, that you haven't yet taken the time to retrain.

It's worth briefly mentioning here that there is danger in gender stereotypes and it's never my intention to imply these stereotypes. For example, it's untrue to suggest that "all men are naturally confident" and "all women naturally lack confidence." Or "all women are emotional" and "all men are non emotive." Neither gender can be put into a box like that. It's dangerous to make these assumptions because they aren't true and could make someone feel like there's something wrong with them. And I would never want that.

## CHILDHOOD—YEP, WE'RE GOING THERE

Most of who we are takes root in our formative years. Even if you had an amazing childhood, I *promise* that you still formed some limiting beliefs along the way. But hold up! We're not here to blame your parents, nor will I spend time in this book blaming my parents.

Even if there are situations where people blamed you and you went through some really horrible and hard things, at this point, you're not allowed to keep pointing the finger at someone else. (If you've gone through a traumatic experience, then I highly suggest you go to therapy and work through it. In fact, I think everyone should go to therapy at some point in their life!)

If you've been in therapy for years and are not seeing the results you're looking for, then maybe it's because you keep pointing the finger. When you constantly point the finger at someone else, you're always playing the victim. You become powerless because you're blaming someone who may never change. You can't sit around and wait for them to change in order for you to grow, all you can do is take personal ownership and responsibility, choose to forgive, and choose to change yourself.

About half of the women I've coached had a really great childhood with two incredibly loving parents who provided for them in every way, just like mine. When I suggest looking into their past, they push back, feeling weird about examining their childhood. They say, "Nothing bad ever happened to me." I respond by letting them know that their experience doesn't have to be this big, horrible, traumatic event. Unfortunately, limiting beliefs can come from the most innocent childhood memories and can have a massive impact on how you're living today.

Let's imagine you were an only child until you were four years old, then your baby sister was born. Maybe you have a memory of being at a party where everyone was giving the baby all the attention. As you were off in the corner feeling lonely, the four-year-old version of yourself created the limiting belief that you are not as lovable as your sister. As you grew older, this manifested into a weird competition with her. You always felt like you weren't quite as good as her.

If you uncover that belief as an adult, you can understand what really went down. Your baby sis was brand new and needed more attention and care. It totally makes sense! But if you never sit still long enough to reflect on your relationship with her, you may not be able to discover the root of the problem. You'll probably wonder why your relationship with her has always had so much tension and continue to fall into the same negative patterns.

To make things even trickier, we look for ways to confirm the limiting beliefs we've created. It's a phenomenon known in psychology as confirmation bias. We're constantly searching for ways to prove that what we believe is true. Maybe you think your parents call your sister more than they call you. Maybe you become jealous of the new job she just got. You've been subconsciously looking for ways to confirm that your little sister is the more lovable one your entire life.

It's like when you're thinking about buying a new car. You test drive that sleek, stunning Tesla and the very next day, all of a sudden, you see more Teslas all around you! Are there more Teslas on the road today than there were yesterday? No, in twenty-four hours Elon Musk didn't dominate the world any more than the day prior. You're simply attuned to and LOOKING for this exact make and model, so you find what you're looking for.

The more you look for ways to confirm your limiting belief, the more true it feels. Eventually you start attracting those types of people or situations into your life and the lie becomes a self-fulfilling prophecy.

Your reality begins to mirror what you're thinking. Your external world is simply a reflection of your internal world.

Another challenge with looking back that I often see is, many women don't remember their childhood at all. It's like a completely blank slate. This is often because they are so new to the art of reflection that reaching that far back feels impossible. So many of us have spent years living our lives at a million miles per hour. We are so freakin' busy that we become numb to what's going on inside of ourselves. Usually people think the only numbing agents are drugs or alcohol. But you can also throw yourself into your career, fitness, social media or a constant state of doing, doing, doing. If we don't *make* the time to process our thoughts and feelings, then *of course* we can't remember anything!

Looking at pictures or video footage of your past can be helpful in jogging some memories. Verbal processing through therapy, especially EMDR (Eye Movement Desensitization and Reprocessing) therapy, is specifically created to support those who have a hard time remembering their past. Sometimes talking to a friend or even speaking out loud into the voice memo app on your phone also works. If I'm driving and obviously can't journal but want to process a thought or journaling prompt, for some reason recording it on my phone seems to be super helpful. You could even do that with the journaling prompts throughout this book!

When reflecting, try to remember a single birthday or a teacher you had one year in elementary school. If you can put your finger on a single detail from your childhood—like your second grade teacher's name—that's a great place to start. Once you have your teacher's name, try to picture the classroom and where you sat. You'll start to pull up memories. Sit with your thoughts as you visualize being in the classroom. Who were your classmates? What snacks did you eat? By thinking hard about these little details, it's like a workout for your brain.

Another way to jog your memory is through journaling. Try sitting in a quiet room with the door closed for twenty minutes and think back to your childhood. Turn off your phone and any technology so you have zero temptations. See if you can remember any details and give yourself permission to write freely. Positive memories. Negative memories. Neutral memories. Give yourself the gift of time to freely reflect and remember.

Lastly, one of the most powerful ways I know to help women remember their past is by sharing stories of my own past. I can't tell you how many dozens of times I've been on a coaching call with a client where I share a piece of my story and the woman listening can relate in some way. It reminds her of something vaguely similar from her past. By sharing my experience, it brings to life a dormant memory that's been sleeping in her unconscious mind. "Wow! I've never really shared this memory with anyone, I didn't realize until just now that this has impacted me all these years," she'll say. And so, me sharing stories from my past is exactly what we will be doing throughout this book.

*Chapter 3*

# A LAUNDRY LIST OF
# LIMITING BELIEFS

After five years of working with women, I've noticed all kinds of common limiting beliefs. Many of the beliefs I'm about to share are etched into our subconscious mind and control our lives without us ever realizing that we've submitted to living under their authority. I've wrestled with many of them and I'm willing to bet some, if not all, of these limiting beliefs will resonate with you too:

- I'm not _____ enough. (I'm not good enough. I'm not outgoing enough.)

- Someone else would do it better. Someone else is already doing it. Or there's lots of people already doing it, the market is already saturated, what would I have to offer?

- I'm too busy! I can't start today but I'll start tomorrow. (Repeating this sentence daily for years on end.)

- I'm bad at confrontation and having hard conversations.

- I'm an outsider. I'm different from other people. People don't like me very much.

- People think I'm annoying. People think I'm "too much."

- I can't have both. I'll either be successful at work or successful at home, having both be successful is impossible.

- I have to work long hard hours to be financially successful.

- I have to do it perfectly. And if I don't, I beat myself up.

- I'm not very smart. Everyone else is smarter than I am.

- Life is so hard for me. Other people just have it so easy.

- I'm not very pretty, I'm kind of the ugly duckling of my friends.

- If I fail I should just give up, it must not be a good fit for me.

- I can't be a leader or impact people's lives because I'm so imperfect and I mess up so much.

- If I really say what's on my mind, I'll hurt other people's feelings or make a fool out of myself so I'd rather say nothing at all.

- I'm just naturally a less confident person. Nothing will ever change that.

- I'll be happy once _____. (Once I lose weight. Once I get the raise. Once I meet my significant other.)

- Either I'm good at something or I'm not. That's just the way that it is. I was born that way.

This list really only scratches the surface because there are thousands of different limiting beliefs that exist. I encourage you to put a star next to the limiting beliefs on that list that you wrestle with and start to pay attention to when your mind thinks those thoughts.

Your limiting beliefs impact every aspect of your life, from your friendships to your mental health, to your bank account and your romantic relationships, to the adventures you allow yourself to experience or your professional opportunities. Limiting beliefs steal our happiness, keep us in negative thought loops, and make us believe we don't deserve to live a life we love. Limiting beliefs make us accept the mediocre and say, "Oh well, this is just the way it is."

So, what's the best way to uncover your limiting beliefs? Glad you asked, girlfriend! The best way I know to uncover your limiting beliefs is by hearing examples of other people's struggles and becoming consciously aware of what thoughts are floating around in *your* mind. A lot of times you won't know it's a limiting belief until you realize you have a choice to think differently. You think that your way of thinking is the only way of thinking because it feels like the truth to you.

But your truth isn't necessarily *the* truth. (That's some ninja inception mind magic stuff, huh?)

Let me give you an example in the form of a jaw dropping ketchup-based thriller:

Let's say your family kept their ketchup in the fridge your entire life. Then one day, you go to your friend Megan's house, and you're about to eat a scrumptious and nutritious hot dog. You head to the fridge and open it up, looking for the ketchup. But dang, you can't find any. You call out to Megs, "Hey, do you guys have ketchup??" And she responds, "Yep! In the the pantry."

Immediately you're like, *Wait what??? How on earth is your ketchup in the pantry? It's supposed to be in the fridge! It's absolutely in the wrong place!!* Your brain can't even compute how or why this family is living their lives like this. *There must be something wrong with this person. That's gross. That's downright wrong!*

You were so ingrained in the way you were raised that it didn't even occur to you that there was another possible place to store ketchup!

Here's another example of awakening to new ways of thinking and living. Let's say you were raised in a middle class family and as a young child, you probably didn't realize your family was classified as "middle class." But in third grade, little Timmy in your class invited you to his ninth birthday party. You were pumped! You headed to the party on a beautiful Sunday afternoon, expecting to arrive at a house that looked similar to your house. But instead, as your mom's car pulled up to the driveway, you saw before your very eyes what seemed to be a mansion! All of a sudden, your little brain was like, "Oh shoot! These people have a much bigger house than ours!"

You walked into this mansion (which is basically a small castle) and you looked around, all bright-eyed and bushy-tailed, thinking, "WHOA. This is crazy. I had NO idea people had houses this big or could afford so many amazing toys!" You simply thought everyone else lived exactly like you. But once you knew differently, your mind expanded and gained awareness of new possibilities.

While the ketchup and the birthday party thrillers may seem somewhat silly and insignificant, they are great examples of a much bigger picture—the way you were raised often puts a subconscious ceiling on what you imagine is possible for your life. But the more you expand your experiences and the more possibilities you begin to see, you realize that if someone else can do it, so can you.

Sometimes these new possibilities seem scary yet inspiring. Sometimes they are motivating. Sometimes your inner voice responds with criticism. Pay close attention to this criticism and know that it's usually covering up a limiting belief. Keep an open mind to explore other possibilities. After all, if after you investigate that other way of thinking or living you end up realizing you preferred your way, you can return to that— this time with clarity and resolve that it was indeed the best way for you.

## ARE YOU GETTING IN YOUR OWN WAY?

Has it ever occurred to you that by not taking action on your audacious dream that you might actually be blocking someone else from their own breakthrough? Maybe it's your best friend, your spouse, your mom, your child, your coworker or even thousands of women and men online. Watching you reach for your biggest dreams and become the healthiest version of yourself will often give others in your life permission to take action towards making their vision a reality too. Your actions will often unconsciously inspire action in others.

(I mean let's be real, there'll be haters too. But you can use the haters' hate to light a fire under your butt and show them what's up!)

But what sucks is that our limiting beliefs often block us from the truest, most grandiose potential for our lives. They stop us from growing into the most badass versions of ourselves, and equally as devastating, they stop us from truly impacting and serving others.

When we start practicing self-belief and speaking kindly to ourselves, it not only influences us, it also affects our family, our spouse, our parents, our children, our coworkers and our friends. We start to become so much more intentional about loving on people and encouraging them the way that we encourage ourselves. We're not threatened by their success because we know there is an abundance of goodness to go around.

So what are the internal battles going on in your mind? What are the whispers you feel inside of you that you're currently ignoring? What lies and limiting beliefs are popping up in your head every time you dream big? Do you find yourself constantly thinking that it's just not quite the right time? Or that you need to be further along in life before you can give something a try?

Sometimes it seems like the older we get, the less qualified we feel.

The older we get, the more we feel the heaviness of failure on our shoulders because we thought we'd be "further along" by now. Let's be honest, the seven-year-old you probably thought you'd be a movie star or astronaut or president at this point in your life! A lot of women I talk to feel their confidence deflate as the years go on because they're disappointed that they haven't accomplished more. There are dreams they keep saying they're going to reach for, but often fear is what's holding them back.

**Some people think that confidence means being fearless, but I don't agree with that. I believe confidence means feeling the fear and doing it anyway.**

Confidence means you have this unshakable trust in yourself to be able to figure it out along the way. So this book isn't to teach you how to become "fearless." I want you to acknowledge the fear, uncover and reflect on the limiting beliefs that are holding you back, and then deliberately choose to speak truth into your life while you do the thing you fear the most.

The truth is, you will never actually feel ready. And you wanna know what's even worse? Your life is probably going to suck a little harder before you get to the amazing reward. It's like you have to take three steps back before you can take ten leaps forward. This process isn't easy.

There's a cheesy mantra that I live by that has helped me punch my limiting beliefs in the face and take risky action on my life: "*Short-term happy face = long-term sad face. Short-term sad face = long-term happy face.*" Let's look at a graphic to make it more fun!

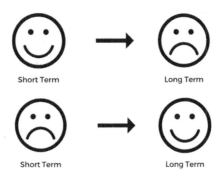

| Short Term | Long Term |
| Short Term | Long Term |

For example, it was absolutely awful when I broke up with my boyfriend of six years in 2014. It broke my heart but it led me to the husband I have today who is everything I ever dreamed of and more, and I'm absolutely obsessed with him.

I could have easily stayed in that relationship. Many women stay, even when they have been unhappy for a very long time. We ignore the whisper because we've invested so much time and energy into the relationship. We don't think we deserve more, or we convince ourselves this is as good as it gets anyway.

Short-term sad face = Long-term happy face.

It was really lonely when I moved to California all by myself in 2016, I cried all the time during the first six months and thought it was a huge mistake! But it eventually turned into an epic adventure and led me to the incredible San Diego lifestyle I live today.

I could have easily stayed in Colorado, thirty minutes away from my hometown. I kept waiting for others to come with me and kept putting it off when they weren't ready. I ignored the whisper that was calling me to try out a new city because I didn't think I was brave enough to make the move alone. But going through that short-term suckiness brought me to where I truly wanted to be.

Short-term sad face = Long-term happy face.

It was terrifying to change my career path approximately seven times, as I fumbled along the way trying to discover where my passion and purpose intersected. I got my degree in Hospitality Management in 2014, and it felt so uncomfortable to officially choose to never use my degree just two years after graduating. I kept thinking, what a waste of money! But each and every job I tried kept leading me closer and closer to my true calling.

I could have given up my search and simply settled down into any of the good jobs I was working. Quitting a bunch of times definitely doesn't look good on a resume. Then in 2018, I quit a job for the final time and started my own business—which seemed like the craziest financial risk in the world. I mean I had five thousand dollars in savings but also an equal amount of credit card debt because I had just hired my first business coach, so it *was* pretty risky. But look where it's led me!

**Short-term sad face = Long-term happy face.**

So I often ask myself, am I choosing a short-term happy face right now? Don't get me wrong, short-term gratification and comfort sure feel wonderful in the moment and there are seasons where I get caught up in that! And it's worth mentioning, I do believe there are seasons where choosing comfort is actually necessary. But I do my best to continually check back in with myself by asking, "In the long term, if I look back on my life in ten years, am I going to be disappointed because I stuck with this thing that I shouldn't have stuck with? Am I going to regret not doing the thing that scares me the most?" Short-term comfort leads to a long-term sad face, and feelings of regret and disappointment.

On the flip side, accepting the discomfort of a short-term sad face, knowing that ten years from now you will be so freakin' proud looking back on your life, will give you the strength and motivation you need to be able to take action on the important things you want most. It's important to take a step back and acknowledge that the situation may suck more at first. But you must have faith that, in a few years, it will lead you to a long-term happy face. And when you are stepping into your purpose, that's the truest happy face!

So what is the big dream for you?

- Is it moving to a new city that makes you feel like the very best version of yourself?

- Is it attracting new, healthy friendships into your life with women who inspire you to level up?

- Is it starting a business and believing that it's going to flourish before you know every last detail?

- Is it becoming a c-suite executive in your current job?

- Is it marrying the man of your dreams?

- Is it working on your money mindset and getting your finances in order?

- Is it saving to buy your first home?

- Is it buying numerous investment properties and having a real estate empire?

- Is it starting a family?

- Is it having a healthy and strong body that you feel good in?

- Is it buying a new wardrobe and making the time to get ready every day so you can feel like the confident woman you are?

- Is it having less stress and more daily peace in your life?

- Is it being able to easily show up to your day with confidence, joy, and lightheartedness?

Then ask yourself—like, get REALLY brutally honest with yourself—what is the short-term sad face that needs to happen today in order to be able to achieve that dream?

## SETTING AN INTENTION

As you read through this book, I want you to become profoundly aware of what limiting beliefs you currently have and how they are holding you back in big and small ways. There will be journaling prompts throughout that I hope you will *actually* make the time to work on. (Don't worry, I trust you to make space for reflection after my whole rant on the importance of reflection earlier!) If you put in the work, this book can indeed change your life.

So without further ado, it's time for you to overcome your limiting beliefs and finally take action on your audacious dreams. It's time to Flex Your Confidence Muscle.

Oh and if you want to share your breakthroughs on social with me and the Next Level Confident Team, please feel welcome to share it and include this hashtag: #flexyourconfidence.

Let's do this thang!!

If you scan this QR code or go to www.nextlevelconfident.com/bookresources you can grab my top resources for confidence growth. I've provided my all-time favorite podcasts, TED Talks, songs, YouTube videos, books and more.

*Part Two*

# UNCOVER YOUR LIMITING BELIEFS

*Chapter 4*

# LIMITING BELIEF: "MAYBE I'M AN OUTSIDER."

While all the other kids in our fourth grade class at Northeast Elementary were at a sex-ed class, I was sitting at a library table with Caitlyn, the one other kid from our class who also wasn't allowed to learn about sex at school.

"I wonder if the horses were exhausted after a long day at work," Caitlyn said to me.

"Yeah. Maybe." I responded, annoyed. *Please for the love of God, just stop talking,* I thought.

"Don't you think it's funny that we're writing about the Pony Express? Like, I wonder why Mrs. Levitsky chose this topic for us?" she continued.

I was getting more frustrated by the minute, "Yep, I know, pretty weird."

I knew I was supposed to be nice to her since everyone else was so mean to her. All the popular girls called her Purple Beaver. I don't remember how that nickname came about but it was definitely not a term of endearment. Kids were so mean to her and it made me really sad. But at the same time I couldn't believe I was stuck spending this time with her every week—just the two of us, alone in the library researching and writing about the freakin' Pony Express.

Plus, I knew our fourth grade teacher Mrs. Levitsky just chose some random thing for us to write about, simply to fill our time since our parents didn't want us to attend the sex-ed class. But *obviously* I wanted to learn all about the sex things with my friends, not study the Pony Express. I felt left out, like a total nerd. I wanted to be with the other kids so badly. I hated being different.

I wasn't surprised that my parents didn't want me to go to the sex-ed class. They thought I was way too young to be learning this kind of content from a random teacher and felt like it was something that should be taught at home at this age instead. Which, looking back as an adult now, I can actually understand. But fourth-grade me felt super ready to learn about whatever it was that all my classmates were learning in the other room.

Up until that year, I was homeschooled, and therefore was dying to release my inner social butterfly at public school. In third grade I started begging my parents to go to this magical thing called "public school" so I could be with all the "cool kids." I wanted to start playing school sports, and to have legit homework, and to show off my new purple sparkly backpack in the fall to people other than my family in our dining room.

My mom, dad, three brothers and I lived in a gorgeous old house built in 1841 in Ithaca, New York—where Cornell University is. I was already well traveled for a nine-year-old. I was born in Kansas, moved to Belarus (which is near Russia) at the age of two, lived there until I was four-and-a-half, when I moved to Colorado for a few months before landing in the beautiful state of New York!

My two best friends in New York were Natalie and Rebekah. Natalie went to public school and Rebekah was homeschooled like me. Rebekah and I would always talk about how we couldn't wait to go to public school. We were both pretty sure we could fit in with the cool kids there because we definitely weren't as nerdy as all the homeschooled kids that we used to hang out with at the weekly co-op. (Now those kids were some serious nerds!)

Anyway, I can't remember exactly when it started, but I know for sure once I got to public school in fourth grade, I was always asking myself this question, "Am I cool enough to fit in?" I wanted to do everything I could to be well-liked, normal and popular. I didn't want to be weird. I didn't want to be different. My goal was to give off Mary-Kate and Ashley vibes every day.

There were so many moments with my friends at school where I thought I stuck out like a sore thumb because I didn't know any of the pop culture they were referencing. I usually tried to fake a laugh with everyone, nod and pretend that I knew what we were talking about. But deep down I was always worried they were going to find out that I was a fake. They'd realize what an outsider I really was.

**How was it that I could feel like too much and yet not enough, all at the same time?**

How was it that in one moment I could tell myself that I was so amazing but the next moment I felt like an awkward weirdo?

Have you felt conflicting feelings like this too?

It was like my true colors were never good enough. I was always pretending to be this confident girl. But on the inside I felt like a loser.

I put up a great front though.

I quickly made friends with all the popular girls. According to my mom, I came home from school one day and announced that I was the second most popular girl in fourth grade, second to the most sought after girl in our grade, this mega cool chick named OT. I thought if I made friends with all of the popular girls, it meant that I fit in, and that their popularity would somehow rub off on me, or something. Even though I felt popular, it always felt like I was one wrong move away from getting kicked out of the "in group," so I constantly made sure I dressed, spoke, and acted the "right way." This insane desire to fit in followed me for a large part of my life, into high school and even college. It took a long time for me to be completely comfortable with my authentic self.

Looking back, I see I had a lot of friends from different walks of life but I never felt like I fully belonged to any one group of people. I think that was a protection mechanism—to stop myself from ever getting hurt by my friends. If I had lots of groups of different friends, and bounced around from friend group to friend group, I would never be at risk of getting hurt. If I felt left out from one group, I could go hang out with a different group, and it felt good to have that safety net.

Everywhere I went, I told myself how much I didn't belong and how I didn't fit in.

I definitely didn't fit in with my church friends. I didn't want to hang out with them outside of church because I felt like they were goody-goodies. They were nice, sweet girls that were so proper. Yuck! I considered myself a Christian, but at the same time, I couldn't stand all the rules and how perfect I felt like I had to be to fit in with that group.

I also told myself that I didn't really fit in with my family. My three brothers were great at following all of our parents' rules and meeting their expectations, and I seemed to be the only problem child. My shorts were always too short, my attitude too defiant. I challenged all of their rules. I knew my parents loved me so much, and I loved them a lot too, but at that time I felt smothered by their love. I wanted to be free to do whatever I wanted to do!

In all these social circles, I had made up my mind that I didn't belong. I wanted so desperately to feel accepted exactly as I was. Instead, I repeated my mantras of choice, mostly on a subconscious level. *I'm an outsider. I don't fully fit in anywhere. No one understands me. No one is like me. I'm just different from everyone else. I don't care what they think, I don't care what anyone thinks. I'll do what I want. I'm strong and independent.*

## LIMITING BELIEF:
## "Maybe I'm an Outsider."

## HOW THIS LIMITING BELIEF MIGHT MANIFEST IN YOUR LIFE...

*Scenario 1:*

If you're telling yourself subconsciously every day "I'm an outsider," this might be your reality.

Let's say a coworker asked you to go to a happy hour with the rest of the team when you first started at your new company, but you immediately thought to yourself: *They don't actually want me to come. This is just a pity invite.* And since nobody wants to be a pity invite, you politely declined.

As time went on, your coworkers stopped inviting you because you declined so many times. Now you really do feel like an outsider! At one point you had an opportunity to be an insider, but you put up your walls and rejected your team without even realizing it. The lie begins to feel more and more true because you attracted that result into your life and your limiting belief became a self-fulfilling prophecy.

*Scenario 2:*

This is on the opposite end of the spectrum. If you desperately want to fit in, instead of pushing people away, you might obsessively try to please and add value to show that you belong. While the behavior shows up differently than the previous scenario, the root lie we're telling ourselves is the exact same: "I'm an outsider."

Maybe you're trying so hard to belong that you've become a YES woman. You say yes to literally everything except yourself—for fear that people will reject you if you say no. Can you volunteer at your kids' school this Thursday? Yes of course! Can you drop the project you're working on and help me with this task on my project? Oh yeah no problem!

Your people-pleasing tendencies often mean you lack healthy boundaries. For example, if you answer work emails at nine o'clock every weeknight and all weekend long, fifty-two weeks of the year. And you volunteer to host all of your friends' birthday parties even though you're absolutely exhausted and no one ever returns the favor. If you have the hardest time saying no to people, your behavior might be attached to this limiting belief. Maybe you have a fear of becoming an outsider.

## ACTION STEPS:

1. **Reflection + Journaling Time:** Can you think back to your experiences in elementary school? Do you remember what labels you had at that age? Were these labels ones that you subconsciously chose or labels that were given to you? Or maybe a combo of both?

Were you Miss Popular or eating your PB&J all alone? Were you labeled because of your weight or because of your gender? Were you labeled because of your ethnicity or socioeconomic status? Did you dislike, or even hate, the labels others gave you? Or did you love the labels you were given—wearing them as a trophy of honor and finding your identity in them?

- **Make a list of five or more labels you received or gave yourself in elementary school.**

  (There can be both positive and negative labels in there. Free flow your ideas and memories, there's no right or wrong way to do this exercise.)

- **Then, ask yourself, which of these labels have stuck with me into adulthood?**

- **Lastly, how do you see these labels impacting you today?**

2. **Healing this limiting belief:** You might be wondering, "What should I do if I'm like one of the women in those two scenarios you described above?" Great question! The first step is to affirm a new truth. The truth is that you are lovable and acceptable exactly as you are today. (See the back of this book

for an extensive list of affirmations.) Any time you hear the lie, "I'm an outsider" pop into your mind, immediately say to yourself "cancel!!" (You can even clap your hands or snap your fingers for a more intense pattern interruption.) Then affirm the truth, even if that truth doesn't feel true yet. You're choosing to speak it into existence. You're manifesting the reality you want to be true. As you intentionally choose to change your mindset, you will naturally start to notice your behavior changing as well.

3. **External Resources:** I really love a book called, *You are Special* by Max Lucado. It's a children's book, but since we're all basically kids stuck in adult bodies, I still believe it's applicable for us. This book talks about positive and negative labels we are given and how we have the power to choose if we're going to let those labels stick or fall off. It's honestly a little bit of a tearjerker because it's just that powerful. On YouTube, you can find an eight minute reading of it. **Put your book down and go watch it now.**

LIMITING BELIEF:
"Maybe I'm an outsider."

THE TRUTH:
I'm an insider. I belong. I am valuable and lovable exactly as I am. It's okay if I don't fit in everywhere I go. I release the need to people please. I am enough just as I am today.

*Chapter 5*

# LIMITING BELIEF: "IT'S COOL TO BE NAUGHTY."

I remember it like it was yesterday. I was sitting at a big round table in the lunchroom of Dewitt Middle School with my best friend Rebekah and our new gal pals, Jordan and Becky. Jordan had her pen and paper out and was making a to-do list to complete after school that day. One of the action items she wrote down was "hide condoms from my parents." She announced this task loud and proud to the table, and the girls began snickering.

I could tell it was something inappropriate that I was supposed to know, so I faked a laugh with the others. I felt like I did a pretty good job acting like I knew what we were talking about, but the wheels in my brain were turning. *What the heck are we laughing at? Why in the world did she need to hide condiments from her parents?? Are they going to be mad that she has her own set of ketchup and mustard???*

Jordan stopped laughing and looked at me with wide eyes, "Oh. My. Gosh. YOU DON'T KNOW WHAT A CONDOM IS, DO YOU??"

*Uh oh. Busted.*

Suddenly, the other girls began laughing even harder. This time, not with me, but *at* me. "You're an innocent little baby," one girl said.

"I can't believe I've ruined a little angel's life!" Jordan said while faking an overly dramatic sad face.

They jeered together. No one stood up for me. They continued to laugh and make fun of my innocence. And me? I felt like the smallest person in the world, like a total idiot. I was mad at myself for being so innocent.

*Why am I so stupid? Why don't I know what they are talking about? What was wrong with me that they all know this joke but I'm too much of a goody-goody to get it? I guess I just don't fit in here. I'm not like the cool girls.*

I remember hating that moment with every fiber of my being. I hated feeling so stupid. I hated my innocence. I hated feeling like the "other." After that, the rumor of me not knowing what condoms were started going around the school and on a regular basis people would call me names like "prude" and "innocent baby."

I decided I never wanted to feel weak or stupid like that ever again. Whatever the opposite of innocent was, that was who I would become! I would prove to them how street-smart and capable I truly was. They didn't know me. I would show them how cool and awesome I would become.

Later that day, I found my other best friend, Natalie, and asked her if she knew what condiments were. She looked at me, confused, and said, "Ketchup and mustard?"

"No. I mean I don't really know. It's something that sounds like condiments but it's something sexual I think?"

"Oooh, condoms!" Her face lit up, and I remember her whispering to me what they were, without an ounce of judgment in her voice. (Sure would have been helpful for my reputation to have been in that sex-ed class, instead of learning about the Pony Express!)

Looking back, this story breaks my thirty-year-old heart. Writing out the details brings tears to my eyes because it was a painful experience for me. I have so much empathy and love for that little twelve-year-old Janelle. She wasn't stupid. She didn't deserve to be laughed at. She didn't do anything wrong at all. She didn't need to put on her armor and go to war. She actually had nothing to prove to this world. But at the time, I didn't know that. I only knew what I knew—that I was an outsider and that it was cool to be naughty.

## PRETENDING TO BE SOMETHING I WASN'T

As a teenager, I was never actually that inappropriate but I purposefully let people think otherwise. I tried to make myself seem like more of a bad girl than I was. If I went to a party in high school, the next day I would talk about our escapades like I was drunker than I really was.

Then in college, a lot of guys on the football team were interested in me and I enjoyed the ego boost of flirting with them. Soon, rumors started going around that I was sleeping with a number of these attractive football players. It was hilarious to me at the time because I knew the truth— not only did I have a long distance boyfriend—I was also a virgin, literally saving sex for marriage! But that didn't matter. I was spicy-bad-girl-Janelle, so I didn't correct people because I thought I would come off more desirable as the woman that had supposedly slept with all of these soon-to-be NFL players.

As you can see, limiting beliefs generally build on top of each other. Like a domino effect. Because I felt like an outsider (from the previous chapter), and I wanted so desperately to be loved and popular, I did the things that it seemed like the "hot girls" were doing. It felt like drinking, partying, boys, and being risqué was the best way to get attention. It felt like the best way to be accepted. So why not pretend and morph into what they wanted?

## LIMITING BELIEF:
### "It's Cool to be Naughty."

## HOW THIS LIMITING BELIEF
## MIGHT MANIFEST IN YOUR LIFE...

*Scenario 1:*

This limiting belief can easily show up in your romantic relationships.

So many single women I've coached tell me they end up having sex really early with a guy they were dating because they feel like they should. Subconsciously a lot of these women believe it's the best way to get the guy to stick around, and to make herself feel loved. But deep down she knows it doesn't feel good in her heart or in her soul. A lot of women think sex is one of their biggest values to a man, but when it's not in the right timing or context, it ends up feeling like they are devaluing themselves. The limiting belief is, "If I don't have sex early on, then the guy is going to leave me!" so she ends up using her body as a way to keep the guy interested.

Some married women pretend to be okay with their husbands checking out other women and making sexual comments about these women and their bodies. Sometimes women even join in the conversation, just to prove how laid back and "cool" they are, even though underneath, these comments are really hurting her and feel super disrespectful. I also know ladies who watch porn with their husbands, even though it makes them uncomfortable and they don't want to. But why do we do it?! Why do we water down our truth to make other people happy? Because as women we're taught from a young age that a man wants a wild woman in the bedroom, even at the expense of our own true feelings about it.

*Scenario 2:*

Have you ever talked crap about someone and then immediately felt horrible about it because the words didn't even feel right as they were coming out of your mouth? Have you ever thought about why you do that?

It's because 99% of the human population likes to use gossip as a false sense of connection! We have all fallen into this trap before so don't you dare pretend like this has never ever happened to you.

Let's say everyone at your office hates the new boss that was just hired, but you actually really like her so far. The next day you're out to lunch with a group of coworkers that are all talking about how awful this boss is. Without even realizing it, because you subconsciously want to ensure that you're fitting in with your pals, you chime in and pretend to dislike the boss and throw a few jabs her way. You'll probably feel kinda bad about it later, but at least you looked edgy and didn't rock the boat, right?

You wouldn't want to be the brownnoser who stands up for the person, because that would mean having to go against the grain. And that would be really uncomfortable. So instead, you pretend to feel something you don't authentically feel. In that moment, you are giving in to the limiting belief "it's cool to be naughty."

## ACTION STEPS:

1. **Reflection + Journaling Time:** Pull out your journal and answer these questions.

Have you ever let people believe an untruth about you because it served you in some way? What benefit did you receive from those lies? How did the lies limit you?

Do you remember a time when you were bullied or made fun of? It might have been from your friends, classmates, a teacher, a sibling, or even a parent. Oftentimes the most hurtful things that are said are jokes from someone who loves us. Sometimes they're quick little jabs that stay with us for years like, "You're scatterbrained. You're always late!"

Write out the story of what happened. Answer the following questions about how you felt, then continue to write freely about the experience.

- Who bullied you or hurt your feelings?

- Where were you?

- Describe the situation.

- What were the lies you began to believe about yourself because of that situation?

- What were the lies you began to believe about the world?

- Make a list of two or three emotions you felt when it happened.

- How do those lies still impact you today?

2. **Healing this limiting belief:** The best way to heal this limiting belief is going to sound repetitive from the previous chapter but it's truly to focus on the things you love about yourself. To find new things to love about yourself. And then choose to forgive the people who hurt you. As you forgive people, you will be able to release the words spoken over you.

3. **External Resources:** This resource will help you get to know yourself better so you can step more into being your authentic self. The Enneagram Personality test! (Pronounced eh-nee-ah-gram.) Go to Truity.com to take a free assessment. After you see your top results, you will need to narrow it down to just one of the numbers. For example, you can't be both a three and a seven. You are only one of those numbers. So then Google 'Enneagram misidentification between 3 and 7", or whichever two you're torn between, and you'll find an article that will help you identify the exact number you are. I would recommend heading to the official Enneagram website, Enneagraminstitute.com, to learn more about your number. If you go down this Enneagram rabbit hole by reading entire pages about your personality type, you'll feel like someone has creepily read your journal and knows way too much about you.

LIMITING BELIEF:
"It's cool to be naughty."

THE TRUTH:
It's cool to be my most authentic self. It's cool to stand up for what I believe in. It's cool to embrace my quirks and weirdness. If we were all the same, the world would be boring. I am proud of who I am.

*Chapter 6*

# LIMITING BELIEF: "IT'S BETTER TO BE NUMB."

"Mary, can I ask you something?" I said in a grown-up voice, feeling empowered by this moment of taking matters into my own hands.

"Of course, what's going on Janelle?" Mary responded.

Mary was my best friend Rebekah's mom. We were hanging out at Rebekah's house and this particular moment in the kitchen felt like the perfect time to bring up the big convo I needed to have with her.

"My parents told me a week ago that our family is moving to Colorado this summer. But here's the thing, I can't go with them. You know? Colorado is so lame! A bunch of farmers and cow people live there. I need to stay here in Ithaca, finish off my last year of middle school, go to high school, and then I'll go to Cornell so I can get a really great education! Anyway, can I live with you all for the next five years until I go to college? I promise I'll help with the cleaning, the dishes, dog training, anything! I really just need a place to stay. And I'll go visit my family in Colorado a lot too! So… yeah. What do you think?"

I took a deep breath of air, since I had basically forgotten to breathe during my entire sales pitch to Mary. Then I sat, eagerly awaiting her response.

"Well, sure," she said slowly, with a grin on her face, "We'd love to have you. But have you spoken with your parents about this idea yet?"

"Okay great!! Awesome!" I was PUMPED. My plan was working out just the way I'd hoped. I knew Mary wouldn't mind having one more kid under her roof. After all, she and her husband had nine kids total—six of them under the age of eighteen and living at home. What was one more?

"And nope, I haven't asked my mom and dad yet, but now that I have a place to live I will talk with them about it! Thank you so much! This is perfect!"

I skipped out of the kitchen and went to go play with Rebekah, my new soon-to-be sister. (I mean it was basically true, now that we would get to live together for the next five years!!)

Later that night, I sat my parents down to break the news. I knew it wouldn't be easy for them to hear that their thirteen-year-old daughter wouldn't be moving across the country with the family and that instead, I would be living in New York with all my friends.

"Mom, Dad, I need to tell you something. I spoke with Mary today and she offered for me to live with her family. That way, I can stay here, in New York. I know it's kinda far from Colorado, but I promise I'll visit all the time and I'll get a cell phone to stay in touch. So, I won't be able to move with you guys to Colorado. I'm sorry, and I'm going to miss you guys a lot, but is it okay with you two that I go ahead and stay here?"

If I'm being honest, I don't remember the looks on their faces while I delivered this information (which felt extremely practical to me). If I were to guess, they likely had their jaws dropped on the ground and eyebrows raised. They probably had to hold back everything in them to not laugh out loud at me, in all my seriousness. Like, nice try, sweet little Janelle.

What I *do* remember is that I did indeed pack my bags and say adios to my home in Ithaca, New York. I moved the summer between seventh and eighth grade to what I deemed a cow town—Greeley, Colorado. And I was NOT happy about it.

When I started at my new middle school in August, I introduced myself to everyone (and I mean everyone!) as Janelle From New York. I did not want a single soul to think I was from this smelly hell hole. I guess I thought that if I kept resisting my reality that maybe it would somehow not be real and everything would go back to the way it was before.

It was around this time that some of my darker thoughts began to take root. I think it was the combo of moving to Colorado, changing hormones, and the limiting beliefs that were already rooted in my subconscious that made these dark thoughts come about. It seems like any time there's a huge life change—especially ones that feel out of your control—there are new limiting beliefs that try to plant seeds in your heart.

## I TOLD MYSELF TO SUCK IT UP!

In eighth and ninth grade, I was low-key angry, but I didn't think I was supposed to feel this way. Other kids seemed happy and like they had it all together, so I hid behind my armor, hoping no one would know how I felt. I would tell myself that my life wasn't that bad, so just get over it. (Which is never actually helpful.)

Here's the thing, when we try to compare our pain to someone else's pain, it's super dangerous. Discrediting any emotions, no matter how inappropriate or uncomfortable, causes you to lose trust in yourself.

I had a client a few years ago who would always brush off her pain—her painful childhood or painful breakups—by quickly referencing things that were much worse, like at least she's not starving and homeless or at least her ex didn't beat her physically, things like that. That's the danger of comparing our pain to other individual's pain. By not validating your own pain, you'll never be able to heal from it. By comparing your pain to other people's pain, you'll always live in a place of comparison, never feeling that your pain or your story truly matters.

That's what I used to do. I would tell myself not to feel pain. *Don't be sad. Don't be angry. You're a happy person, your life is fine, suck it up!*

**Brené Brown says you can't numb the bad without also numbing the good.**

I think eighth grade was when I started learning the art of numbing. My life anthem was "sticks and stones may break my bones but words (and emotions) will never hurt me." I figured if I told myself that often enough, it would start to feel true. Which is actually somewhat accurate. Whatever you tell yourself long enough WILL eventually turn into truth.

## MY DARKEST SEASON

It was in this season of my life that I started to think about disappearing. I don't remember the exact moment when the thoughts began though I do remember one of the moments that felt the darkest.

In our house in Greeley, Colorado, I had a beautiful room all to myself. I loved my room, and to be honest, I often locked myself in that room to get away from everyone. My parents had bought me this cool, white, tall sleigh bed and it felt really regal. On top of it, was this awesome pink comforter from the store Tuesday Morning that I remember picking out myself—and my mom agreed to purchase! Best of all, it was from the brand Seventeen. I'm pretty sure I wasn't even allowed to read the Seventeen magazine but boy did I feel grown up purchasing a Seventeen comforter!

Because the bed was so tall, there was a lot of space underneath it. My childhood dog, Huckleberry (also known as Huckle Buckle) would sleep under that bed because he loved to be near me. There would be times when he would be under there and a friend would be over, hanging out in my room. He would come sauntering out and the friend would let out a little scream because she had no idea there was an animal hanging out with us in the room too.

There were a few occasions when I would come home from school feeling especially lonely, frustrated and angry, and I would shimmy my teenage body underneath that bed, into the farthest corner where Huckle usually slept. I would curl up in the fetal position and cry. I would cry really, really hard. I never wanted anyone to see me cry or hear me cry. It was far too private to bring out in the open, because I believed crying was weak.

The moment that stands out most was a day when I was under my bed, crying, and I started thinking about stories I'd heard about some kids at school who would cut themselves. They would take a razor to their skin and make cut marks on their wrist. Sometimes they would do it in more discreet places so the marks weren't so obvious. When I heard kids talk about it, I didn't understand why they would hurt themselves like that. But for whatever reason, on this particular day, I started thinking it sounded really nice to try out this whole cutting thing. I wondered what it would feel like to inflict that kind of pain on myself.

I can't remember my motive in wanting to try it. Was it to relieve my own emotional pain? Was it because I was hoping that someone would see it and I could talk about it and get attention?

As I sobbed uncontrollably under the bed that day, I took my finger nail, and began to aggressively scratch lines on my forearm, wondering if I could cause myself to bleed.

All of this was a manifestation of how unwilling I was to talk about my emotions.

I wasn't willing to acknowledge the pain. I wasn't willing to be vulnerable enough to let anyone into my mess because I was too embarrassed. I wanted to be strong enough to do it by myself.

As the months went on, dark thoughts were playing in my mind with increasing repetition. I fantasized about my disappearance more and more. It was in those vulnerable moments—by myself, laying under the bed, or laying on top of my bed right before drifting off to sleep in the darkest hours of the night—that my mind went wild. I would replay all of my interactions from the day. Who said what to me.

What was meant by it. And while the constant over-analyzing was exhausting, the vicious loop felt uncontrollable.

I would have NEVER told anyone that I was depressed, and I certainly wouldn't have ever identified with the word suicidal. I wouldn't have even admitted that word to myself because I honestly didn't realize how dark my thoughts were. I was living in denial. (Plus, I was "just" thinking about harming myself. And just thinking about how I could disappear off the face of this earth. And if I were to take my own life, how might I do it? But that's not depressed, right? Wrong.) This denial kept me numb and feeling my true emotions seemed basically impossible. But I sure looked happy on the outside.

I saw a TikTok recently that showed a video of a beautiful girl who was laughing, dancing and seemed so genuinely happy, and the words said, "this video was taken twelve hours before my best friend took her own life." The next words that flashed across the screen were, "Check on your happy friends too." That video hit home for me because that was my life, minus the fact that I never followed through with it. And I'm blessed to be living to write this book. But I was the "happy" friend. Absolutely no one really knew what went on in my mind.

## THE UNBELIEVABLE ESCALATION

At first I started envisioning a fairly innocent running away story. (I think there were probably some Mary Kate and Ashley movies where they ran away from home or something so it felt cute and adventurous.) It sounded nice not to worry about fitting in anywhere. I didn't know where I would go, but I enjoyed thinking about my parents calling the cops, the drama that would ensue, and the kids at school finding out that Janelle Huskerson had disappeared. *Gasp*. I imagined the rumors going around the school about where I had gone. Every lunchtime conversation, every bus ride, everyone talking about me and how I'd gone missing and where the hell did she go?! I enjoyed thinking about the attention that would follow. I pictured myself somewhere far, far away where I could somehow watch and listen to all those conversations about me, and I got a smug feeling knowing they were all missing me. I knew once I disappeared they'd start to realize how awesome I was all this time.

If you've ever had a creepy daydream while picking at your split ends, or viciously scrubbing burnt eggs off the bottom of a pan, you'll know what I'm talking about here. We go to these weird, weird places in these daydreams where we picture worst case scenarios playing out, and we go into so much detail in the visualization that it actually starts to feel quite real. We might even start to feel the emotions we would feel if it really happened.

This is what I would do with my disappearing visualization. It felt so wrong to picture it all, but at the same time it felt so good to imagine the story playing out. As time went on, these daydreams got worse. I started to think about how much more drama would be stirred up if I were to actually die. Disappearing would be crazy, but death would be even crazier. Then it would be a permanent goodbye that they said to me. At first it started like a fun idea, like Tom Sawyer faking his own funeral and watching everyone who attended. Innocent enough right? As this daydream continued, I knew a fake death wouldn't do. It needed to be a real death.

Boy did I love envisioning my funeral! It was a packed house! People would come from near and far to celebrate my incredible life. In fact, there would be so many people that there wasn't enough space in the main church auditorium. They would have to have an overflow room, where people would watch the funeral on a screen, just like when popular pastors preached at our church.

The popular girls would go up to my parents and would grossly exaggerate our friendship—because of course they wished they had become best friends with me and now that I was dead they felt bad they hadn't given me more of a chance. They would tell my mom and dad how much they loved me, how cool I was, and would share epic memories we had together.

And then here's where things got REALLY messed up in my head. Super twisted.

I had been to a few funerals at this point, and every time I went to a funeral, the person or pastor who was leading the whole thing would always mention God a bunch of times. They'd talk about God's love and how the person went to heaven and was in a better place now, and was happy now. Of course I pictured myself in heaven, feeling no more pain, no more sadness, and feeling 100% happiness in the presence of God. But the crazy part was, I figured my funeral would be a revival of sorts.

Since hundreds of people were there, and the pastor would talk about God, I imagined that everyone who wasn't a Christian would actually be so moved by the ceremony and the loss of this young girl's life, that they would definitely give their life to God! Then I would be forever a part of their God story, which felt like such an honor. In my mind, I was actually being sacrificial like Joan of Arc. I had it in my head that none of those people would come to know God unless I died and had this epic funeral.

So the worst part of all these dark thoughts was that I actually thought God wanted me to die for my friends and family because it would bring more people to him. I would picture how bittersweet the whole thing would be because they would all be missing me so much, but then they'd find a relationship with God.

## "CRAZY" THOUGHTS & NUMBNESS

Now maybe you've never pictured your funeral —(and I really hope you haven't! If you have, hopefully you pictured yourself at the age of ninety-five, dying after a beautiful long life. Unfortunately, the more I've told this story publicly on podcasts and in speaking engagements, the more I've had people reach out and share their own fear of dying young or their belief that they should die in the near future. Sometimes people tell me they've envisioned what would happen if they had cancer. I spoke with a young gal from Australia who shared that she had a dream once of a tombstone with a date that was three years in the future. She believed this dream was destined to come true.

No matter what, I'm willing to bet you've had some other weird thoughts that are a bit dark. Talking to women and finding out what thoughts they ruminate on is my full-time job and trust me, I've heard it all.

Maybe you've pictured your husband cheating on you, or that he actually has an entire other family in another city that you don't know about. Maybe you've played out scenarios of what it would be like if your best friend was actually a murderer and is wanting to kill you and your kids. You guys, these are real irrational fears I've heard out of the mouths of women I know and I've worked with and while I obviously don't wish any of these thoughts—and definitely not that reality—on anyone, I DO wish it was more normal to talk about these kinds of "crazy" fears. In fact, in general I wish it was more normal to talk about how imperfect life is. Then we wouldn't feel so scared when we have these negative thoughts and feelings.

But because we live in a society that glorifies perfection and happiness and success, we think there's something wrong with us when we have weird thoughts or bad days or hard seasons of life. And so the second we feel negative feelings like isolation, abandonment, grief, shame, jealousy, bitterness, fear, anxiety, rejection, overwhelm, sadness, or anger, we immediately go into numbing mode to pretend we don't feel those things. Numbness feels safer than feeling dark feelings.

Numbness is a survival strategy that keeps us from thinking about our lives. When we get quiet and reflect, we can hear our own thoughts and, sometimes, we don't like what we hear. Am I truly happy? Am I pursuing things that I want to pursue? Are my relationships healthy? Do I like what I'm doing with my life and my career? Do I feel like I'm growing as a human? Do I have dreams that I'm not fulfilling?

At one personal development conference I went to, they put it like this:

- What are you pretending not to know?
- Read that sentence again.
- What are you pretending not to know?
- Frickin' mic drop right there.

## LIMITING BELIEF:
### "It's Better to be Numb."

## HOW THIS LIMITING BELIEF MIGHT MANIFEST IN YOUR LIFE...

You might be numbing yourself if you...

- Can't spend thirty minutes alone without distraction or achievement (calling a friend, scrolling social media, watching TV, listening to a podcast)

- Are constantly answering emails every single night of the week, at family gatherings or your kid's Saturday morning soccer game

- Can't sit still (example: obsessively cleaning)

- Are driven by productivity and the thought of an unchecked box on the to-do list stresses you out

- Are constantly busy and stillness or relaxing freaks you out

## ACTION STEPS

1 **Reflection + Journaling Time:** Begin observing your thoughts daily. As different thoughts go through your mind, acknowledge them. Awareness is necessary for change. Hopefully you can't relate to my thoughts of death, but I'll bet you've had some pretty strange thoughts once or twice. Pay attention to dark, weird, or simply negative thoughts that flash across your mind.

Give yourself grace for the thoughts that aren't positive. Toxic positivity is dismissing all negative emotions and never giving yourself empathy. Your negative thoughts don't define you. I challenge you to look your darkest, most negative thoughts in the eye. When we acknowledge our thoughts we take away their power and set ourselves free.

- Grab your journal and jot down thoughts you notice yourself having today as you go about your day. See if you can come up with five thought patterns, specific words or sentences you're repeating internally over and over again.

- Make a list of three to five ways that you find yourself filling your time to stay busy.

- Begin to pay attention to times where you might be choosing busyness as a way to numb an emotion, thought or fear you're struggling with. When this temptation kicks in, resist it, and instead set a timer on your phone for fifteen minutes that says for the next fifteen minutes you're not allowed to "do" anything. No technology. No work. Nothing. You can only "be" for fifteen minutes. Sit with your thoughts in silence. I don't care if you have to lock yourself in the bathroom for this exercise. Get still. Ask yourself: What am I avoiding right now? What am I feeling? Is there anything I can do to heal this situation or is this something I simply have no control over and must release?

## 2   Healing this limiting belief:

Four Steps to Getting Out of a Funky Mood:

- **Step 1:** Acknowledge that it's okay to not be positive all the time. We all experience weird moods, off days, etc. This is the human experience. Give yourself grace.

- **Step 2:** Name the negative emotions you're feeling. I find it most helpful to look at a feelings wheel that has a hundred different emotions on it so I can get specific with naming them. If you google "Emotions Wheel" a bunch will pop up. I highly recommend this.

- **<u>Step 3:</u>** Get curious about what might have triggered those emotions. I like to journal all the things that are pissing me off and get super dramatic with it too.

- **<u>Step 4.</u>** Only once I've validated my emotions do I allow myself to change my state. I listen to an uplifting podcast or a song or YouTube video to pick me back up!

3 **External Resources:** This song is one of my all time favorite songs: "Rejoice" by Steve Angelo & T.D. Jakes. One of my clients told me it's one of the main things she took away from our coaching together. (Which is kind of funny because obviously she received a lot of other tools as well but she started listening to this song everyday and the words were really powerful for her!)

On a more serious note, if you are struggling with mental health and need support, know that people are here for you. There is absolutely no shame in getting professional help. I wish I would have gotten help sooner.

**National Suicide Prevention Lifeline 1-800-273-8255**
They are available twenty-four hours
and speak English, and Spanish.

**To find an online therapist, go to BetterHelp.com.**

**To find a therapist in your local area, go to PsychologyToday.com.**

LIMITING BELIEF:
"It's Better to be Numb."

THE TRUTH:
It is safe for me to feel a full range of emotions. It's safe for me to slow down. I love myself on good days and on the bad days. I release the need to pretend I have it all together. I choose to share my feelings with trustworthy people.

# Chapter 7

# LIMITING BELIEF: "MY BODY IS WHAT MAKES ME BEAUTIFUL."

It was freshman or sophomore year of high school when I became acutely aware of my butt. Acutely aware of the size of it, the shape of it, and that boys liked it. I remember the day my guy friend Max told me that I had been deemed the girl with the best butt at school. And since I was still pretty innocent when I found out, I was actually very confused about what it meant to have "a nice butt." Like butts are gross! You poop out of those things! Why the heck are people looking at them and saying they're nice?? It was so weird, so uncomfortable to even think about it.

After that, I felt like everywhere I went people would comment on my butt. Even my girlfriends would tell me they wanted a butt like mine. One time, when I was sixteen or seventeen, I went to a party where my nickname for the night was "end table ass"—which apparently means you can set a drink on the top part of my butt, the way you can put a drink on an end table? I honestly still barely get it to this day. Very weird.

And while there was a part of me that liked the notoriety and compliments about this butt of mine, there was this other part of me that was just confused and to be honest, felt a little violated. Deep down, I didn't really like everyone looking at my body like that. It felt inappropriate. But on the surface, it seemed cool to have this butt that people wanted, and it made me feel sexy.

Because of this, and because I was a pretty girl in general, I started to find a lot of my self-worth and identity in my body at a young age. I started to see that guys liked me more because of my body and my beauty. They flirted with me and wanted to hang out with me. There was a part of me that started to wonder if they liked my body even more than they liked my personality.

And because I believed the lie that I wasn't cool enough, the popular girls didn't *really* like me, and that I was living in the shadow of other people, my body and beauty felt like the thing that often gave me validation. Afterall, I had a better butt than the popular girls at least!

It's a lot of pressure to feel like your body has to look a certain way in order for you to be loved, admired and desired. It's a lot of pressure to feel like your beauty is what gets people to like you.

We are inundated with messaging about what our bodies are "supposed" to look like. We see gorgeous bodies on TV, perfectly posed selfies in our social media feeds, and perfectly toned models on magazine pages while we wait in line at the grocery store. We constantly talk about our weight and figure in conversations with our best friends and often make comments about it throughout the day without realizing it.

**Think about the messages you received as a child from your family members.** Think about the way your own mom talked about her body when you were a little girl and as a teenager. Did she talk about how she didn't like her weight? How she needed to be more careful about what she ate? That she's starting a new diet tomorrow? One of my clients told me that her mom even said, "No man wants a heavy wife." Like… WHAT?! These are the messages we're hearing from all sides.

I'm also willing to bet that there have been older women in your life who warn you about the ominous future of your body as the years go on. They say, "It's so easy for you right now. You're so young! It's going to get a lot harder to keep the weight off when your hormones change." When you hear someone say that kind of thing, you can't help but think, *I'm not going to be able to maintain this body. It's gonna go downhill from here.*

I can't even tell you how often I have conversations about body image with my clients. Short women, tall women, curvy women and slender women—each one is so very concerned about how she looks. It's like we can't win!

Whatever your body shape is, most of us compare ourselves to other women and wish we looked more like someone else. If you're naturally thinner, you look at more muscular or thicker women and wish you could have a body (or a booty!) like that. If you're naturally more muscular or thicker, you want to be thinner and have less body fat and have a "thigh gap." It all makes me so sad. **The grass isn't always greener, ladies.** And what makes me even more sad is that even the youngest children are surrounded by this negative messaging and begin to compare themselves at a ridiculously early age.

A few years ago, one of my clients shared that she felt unlovable because her body wasn't ideal. She couldn't remember a time that she DIDN'T feel that way. She could think back to how much she hated P.E. in first grade because she thought her legs were fat. She would feel uncomfortable wearing shorts to class because she didn't want anyone to look at her chubby legs. She was six years old!

When we grow up learning limiting beliefs about our bodies and our beauty, it not only shatters our ability to love ourselves, but it breeds negativity and jealousy in our relationships with other women. I have found that the more harshly a woman judges her *own* body, the more critical she is of *other people's* bodies. If a woman is constantly obsessed with lowering her own body fat percentage, she can't help but constantly look at other people's body fat percentage because it's always on her mind. We can't just point our fingers at men and say they're womanizing us by looking at our butts and our boobs and telling us we need to look a certain way. Women are just as hard, if not harder on each other.

Be honest, have you ever thought or said any of the following?

- She shouldn't be wearing that.
- Did you see her take a second helping of dessert?
- Too much makeup, honey.
- Are you sure you want to eat that?
- Yikes, she's really putting on a lot of weight lately.

I don't believe any of us—well, at least most of us—are purposefully being mean. We simply learned this way of thinking and being from society and now we think it's normal to body shame ourselves and others. But in reality, these little digs and judgments come from a place of scarcity and fear. As long as we see someone else who is not as fit, beautiful or well dressed as we are, then we feel a sense of satisfaction. We feel validated when we put her down because it subconsciously elevates us. It's a way of constantly one-upping each other.

## SCARCITY VS. ABUNDANCE

Have you ever been in a workout class and found yourself comparing your body to the fitness instructor's body? As you are lunging and squatting away, you catch yourself thinking, "Dang, she's so fit. Look at her arms! They're super sculpted.

I feel like mine are pretty flabby compared to hers." Instead of enjoying your class, you are now thinking she's the clear winner, which then makes you feel like the loser. Scarcity, as though there can only be one hot mama in the studio. Or only one body type can be deemed as beautiful.

WebMD defines a scarcity mindset as, "when you are so obsessed with a lack of something—usually time or money— that you can't seem to focus on anything else, no matter how hard you try." Scarcity is saying we can't all be winners, so either she has to win or you have to win. The natural instinct, then, is to keep looking around the workout class to find someone whose body is a little worse than yours. Phew! Okay great, found one. Now you feel better.

Once you begin to unpack the limiting beliefs scarcity brings about, it's obvious that you want nothing to do with that load of horse poo. So the next step is to shift your mindset to focus on abundance. We are all beautiful and badass in our own way! There's room in this world for all of us to be hot mamas! There's room in this world for every body type to be accepted.

I suggest that whenever you notice that you're feeling jealous toward someone else and begin to feel less than her, turn it into a compliment for her AND for you. "My trainer looks incredible! But do you know what? So do I! I've been working out really hard lately and DAMN I look good!" (Even if you don't FULLY believe this compliment you're giving yourself, for the millionth time, keep saying it. You are speaking your new reality into existence.)

The cool thing is that this abundance mindset can be transferred to other areas of your life. If there's a woman that's a total boss in your meeting today, you can choose to think, "She's so successful! But wow I'm really successful too, otherwise I wouldn't be sitting in the same room as her." You don't have to be intimidated by her. Not everything has to be a competition. You are both allowed to be successful.

> Focusing on abundance allows you to release control and stop feeling so threatened by the beauty, intelligence or talent of others.

One of my clients told me she used to be super annoyed when certain coworkers shared ideas and opinions in meetings, and she'd constantly try to think of a better idea than them so she could feel more valuable to the team. After consciously shifting her mindset (via a coaching session and putting a sticky note reminder that says "ABUNDANCE" on her computer) she now has started to welcome these awesome ideas from coworkers.

She realizes that their awesome idea doesn't mean she's going to lose her job for not being good enough at that moment. She no longer feels the pressure about having to produce a better idea than everyone else. Both can share great ideas and both can be winners. Now, she loves brainstorming with her coworkers. She feels at ease and she's having more fun at work!

It's INSANE how much a scarcity mindset can limit us in every area of our life. For example, for the longest time, I had a bottle of my favorite perfume that I would only let myself wear on super nice occasions. I would think, "Oh, it's too expensive. I don't want to waste it." And when I did wear it, I would be like, "Two sprays only, Janelle, don't use too much!" Then years would go by and my precious perfume would go bad. I'd have to throw out a half full bottle because it didn't even smell good anymore. It was actually sad.

About a year ago, I treated myself to a more expensive bottle of perfume than I'd ever bought before (Le Labo!) and promised myself that I would wear it every single day. I called it my "Abundance Perfume." I also made myself stop counting the sprays! I told myself that I was worth it and gave myself permission to use it with abundance. And you know what? Wearing it makes me feel beautiful and luxurious FOR ME, I don't wear it for anyone else. So wear whatever makes you feel luxurious and abundant every single day—a gorgeous piece of jewelry, a full face of makeup, your favorite designer purse, or an awesome outfit from Target. Feel beautiful for *yourself*, not for anyone else.

## IS YOUR BODY IMAGE GETTING IN YOUR WAY?

One of my clients dreamed of starting her own personal development brand on Instagram. She wanted to be the next Rachel Hollis and she was totally capable of it. The problem was, she kept focusing on her body. "I can't be all over social media until I lose fifteen pounds. I can't get started on my brand until my body looks better."

I have a friend who kept herself out of the dating scene because she wasn't happy with her weight. This girl is crazy smart, kind-hearted, and super successful! She's a real catch but she didn't feel that way.

**What are you putting off because you are constantly putting focus on your body (when it should be on more important things)?**

And how badly are you beating yourself up instead of loving on yourself?

So many women (myself included, in the past) use harsh self-talk as a form of motivation. We boot camp ourselves into a workout. We're like, "Get your lazy ass off that couch and go for a run! Do you want to get fat?" Or, "Girl, if you eat that cookie, you will need to do 100 sit ups tonight." We're so harsh on ourselves and our motivation comes from a place of shame and guilt.

But what if we chose to workout and take care of our bodies from a place of self-love? What if we moved our bodies and ate healthy food because we are so incredibly grateful for the beautiful body we have today?

The motivated self-talk in that moment would then sound like, "Girl, I believe in you. Get up off this couch and go lift some weights for thirty minutes. You got this! You're going to feel so good and so strong afterwards!" Or, "Yum! I am

LIVING for this cookie. How is it so gooey and delicious?!!"
And that's all. Because you don't need to be thinking about
your next workout when you eat a treat. When you're
balanced and practicing self-love, eating healthy sounds
great, enjoying treats in moderation feels natural, and any
unhealthy weight easily falls off.

## WHAT REALLY MATTERS

Does it really matter what size you are or how much you
weigh? Does it actually matter what shape your butt is or
how good your hair looks? NO! It certainly doesn't matter as
much as we like to pretend it does. So why are we wasting so
much of our precious time and mental space focusing on this?!

When we look good, we feel good, so I think it's important
to take care of ourselves physically. I want you to feel strong,
to find joy in your body, to love looking at yourself in the
mirror, to feel energetic. I want you to choose healthy
habits, to make time for your wellbeing, and to live a long,
flourishing life.

Before I share some helpful tools to shift your body image
mindset, it's important to think about your own limiting
beliefs when it comes to how you look.

### LIMITING BELIEF:
### "My body is what makes me beautiful."

## HOW THIS LIMITING BELIEF
## MIGHT MANIFEST IN YOUR LIFE...

*Scenario 1:*

Maybe you are the person who steps on the scale every morning and the number that looks back at you determines how your day will go. Maybe you have a goal weight and think you'll be more desirable, more lovable once you get there. You use your weight as a measure of success and that number has a vice grip around your neck. You'll know you can be happy with yourself once you hit that magical number.

*Scenario 2:*

Maybe you find yourself canceling on social outings with your friends or deciding not to go to the party last minute because you can't find anything in your closet that looks good on you. You tried on a hundred different outfits but told yourself your body looked awful in all of them. You'd rather stay home and hide than feel like the fat friend. Or maybe you do go, but you opt for wearing the baggiest outfit you can find, hoping no one will notice your body behind all the fabric.

## ACTION ITEMS:

1 **Reflection + Journaling Time:** Make a list of all of the negative messages you heard in childhood and in your teenage years about weight and beauty. Rewrite them as the truth.

2 **Healing this limiting belief:** First of all, I highly recommend throwing out your scale. I threw mine out

years ago and it was liberating. If you're not willing to do that yet, start by decreasing how often you weigh yourself. If you're weighing yourself every day right now, decrease it to one time per week. One way to ensure you're not tempted to step on the scale more than once a week is to pick an exact day and time each week, like Thursday mornings at seven o'clock for example, and promise yourself you won't get on it at any other time. Of course if you end up getting on less, that's a huge win. Watch how much happier you feel every day as you release your detachment to that number!

**Next**, become intentional about the language you use and try to use words that show yourself and others love and respect. Some examples include saying "slender" instead of "skinny" and "curvy" instead of "fat."

**Then**, start following body positive social media accounts and unfollow accounts that make you feel like crap. Even if the woman you're following is a friend or a positive influencer, it doesn't matter. If her posts trigger you to feel bad about your body, unfollow. You can always choose to follow her back in a different season of your life.

**Lastly**, stand in front of the mirror and use positive affirmations. I know this one seems cringy but it's so powerful. Instead of looking at yourself and focusing on your weight, your acne, your wrinkles, or your stretch marks, tell yourself how much you love your body and that you are beautiful.

Affirmations work like a placebo. When you say something out loud over and over again, it tricks your brain into believing it. Maybe you've heard of auto-suggestion, which Wikipedia defines as "the hypnotic or subconscious adoption of an idea through the repetition of verbal statements to oneself in order to change behavior." So, when you are standing in front of the mirror, checking yourself out, try these affirmations on for size:

- My body is strong.
- I enjoy looking at my body.
- I am athletic.
- I am powerful.
- I am beautiful.
- I love myself.

3   **External Resources:** Head on over to YouTube and search "You're More Beautiful Than You Think" by Dove Real Beauty Sketches. The 6:36 minute one is the best. Get ready for another tear jerker.

When it comes to affirmations, Louise Hay is one of the OGs. Check out her video "Affirmations for Loving Your Body" on her HealYourLife channel. It's thirty-six minutes of the most soothing voice and energy you've ever experienced!

For more on scarcity and abundance, I highly recommend reading *You Are a Badass at Making Money* by Jen Sincero.

LIMITING BELIEF:
"My body is what makes me beautiful."

THE TRUTH:
My mind, personality and spirit is where my true beauty lies. I am beautiful inside and out. I release the need to impress others with my looks. I am abundant. I am worthy of love no matter what I look like. I'm proud to take up space physically, mentally and emotionally.

## Chapter 8

# LIMITING BELIEF: "I'M NOT SMART ENOUGH... YET."

My older brother Austin and I are fifteen months apart. When we were homeschooling, he and I did a lot of learning together. That's when I got the first hint that school was maybe a bit easier for him than it was for me. This became really obvious when we went to public school because he had harder classes than I did and got better grades. On top of that, he was a year ahead of me and he used to remind me of it constantly. He'd be like, "Janelle, you think you know sooo much, but you're only in third grade! I'm in fourth grade and when you get to fourth grade, you realize how little you knew in third grade."

And I would think, *Okay yeah, that makes sense. When I get to fourth grade, I'll know a lot too.* Except, I'd get to fourth grade and Austin would say, "Just wait until you get to fifth grade, Janelle. Then you'll really start to get it!"

I was always trying to catch up to my brother—to be older and smarter—but I was always behind.

In elementary school, there's this thing called Accelerated Reading (AR). It's a computer program that I don't think was ever mandatory, but probably exists to measure your reading skills. Or to gamify reading to trick kids into thinking it's fun. Anyway, you pick a book to read, then you answer a quiz on the computer to test your comprehension. Do you remember that? I always chose easier, more fun books like Mary Kate and Ashley mysteries. They weren't worth many AR points because, let's be honest, they weren't very challenging to read. Austin, on the other hand, would read the Harry Potter books. They're HUGE, thick books, and probably have big words too or something, so they're worth more points. Like, A LOT of AR points.

One day, I convinced my brother to take an AR test on the Harry Potter books under my name. I got so many points that a few weeks later I was called up to the front of the gymnasium at the school assembly so the principal could give me a blue ribbon. (Blue ribbons are the best ribbons, in case you forgot.) You guys, I had no guilt! I was so pumped!

I can't remember how my dad found out, but when my brother and I got home after school, he wasn't happy. My dad marched me back to my classroom, put his hand on my shoulder and made me hand that blue ribbon back to my teacher because

I had cheated. Okay, it was a powerful parenting moment and I'm proud of my dad for teaching me about honesty and integrity that day, but at the time, it was pretty horrifying. I had a lump the size of a toad in my throat as I fought back tears of embarrassment, pissed to give up my awesome blue AR ribbon.

Looking back, it makes me sad because I can see my limiting belief of not being smart enough show up in this memory. I thought I needed to use my brother for his smarts. I didn't believe I was capable of authentically earning the blue ribbon on my own. And that was a lie I believed for way too long. In fact, it's still one that I'm working on. I'd be lying if I told you that I don't still struggle with this one today.

One of my clients, Abigail, put it this way on a recent coaching call, "I feel like I have this belief that I have to ride on the coattails of other people's success because I'm not smart enough to be successful all on my own." Wow. That summed up my limiting belief PERFECTLY too.

## CONFIRMATION BIAS

We touched on this phenomenon briefly at the beginning of the book and I want to dive deeper into it now. Confirmation bias as told by Wikipedia is, "the tendency to search for, interpret, favor, and recall information in a way that confirms or supports one's prior beliefs or values."

**When we form a belief, our brains have the amazing ability to find confirmation everywhere.** If you think you're short, you will notice tall people all around you. If you think you're no good with money, you will notice others who seem to have an abundance and are living the life of your dreams. If you think you aren't smart enough (like me) you perceive all kinds of messages that confirm your lack of intelligence.

For example, I received such a message at my volleyball awards banquet my senior year of high school. As my volleyball coach called up the athletes, one by one, she'd say something nice about them as she handed out the trophies. "This award goes to Heather. We love her enthusiasm and drive. She's got the best spike in the league." When she called my name, all she said was, "This is Janelle... She asks a lot of questions."

Everyone laughed.

Now, she may have said other things too, but I only remember that single sentence. Because I believed I wasn't smart, I took this comment as confirmation. I asked a lot of questions because I didn't know much. I was stupid.

Was this what my volleyball coach actually meant? I have no idea. Probably not, but it doesn't really matter. If I was confident and thought I was smart, I would have heard that comment and thought, *Dang right I ask a lot of questions! They say that's a sign of intelligence. Curious people are super smart, so I must be a freaking genius! I probably have quite the high IQ!*

And you know what? Even if she DID mean that comment as a low-key dis, if I was confident and believed I was smart, I wouldn't have felt triggered at all. I would be able to look at the comment from a subjective standpoint and have a level of detachment around her opinion of me. Who cares what she said? I know I'm smart and I love the question-asker that I am. She doesn't get to have that power over me. You see the difference?

Now, when someone makes a comment that might be interpreted as rude, instead of overthinking it, I simply let it go. Maybe that person likes me, and maybe they don't, and either way, that's okay. It's actually none of my business what they think of me. And now when people are downright disrespectful or mean to me, I actually feel sad for them because I know that they are incredibly insecure so they feel the need to put other people down. Then I generally end up trying to send love their way, because I know that person doesn't have enough love in their life. Anyway, I digressed. Where were we?

## HONORING YOUR UNIQUE TALENTS

When I look back on myself as a little girl, I can see that I was different from Austin. We were both smart, just in different ways. He was really studious and naturally more book smart, while I was running around in the backyard pretending to be a unicorn with my friends. I was artistic, always coloring and writing little books and those activities seemed silly. I can see *now*, that imagination was my gift. This same creativity has served me well as an entrepreneur because I can think outside of the box and be innovative. As a girl, all I saw was that my brother was smart and I wasn't. So I thought, if he is "the smart one" I might as well be "the fun one."

I leaned into that persona, especially during my college years when I was partying and living a double life. I drank so much that I ended up in the hospital one night, but at the same time I would go to church like I knew I "should." Because I believed I would die young and that I wasn't that smart, it didn't really matter what degree I earned. I didn't put any serious effort toward my education. I lived in the moment, not thinking about the future. Had I known that "smart" comes in many shapes and sizes, I may have tried a little harder to succeed. Had I known that my life actually matters and was meant to live with purpose, I would have done things differently.

The TRUTH is that we are all smart—creatively, socially, academically, musically, mathematically, analytically, and the list goes on. We each come to this earth with beautifully unique talents that should be celebrated. I believe with every fiber of my being that every single human on earth is incredibly smart and has original value to offer this world. I really want you to hear this, because I see women struggling to value their own intelligence all the time.

## LIMITING BELIEF:
### "I'm Not Smart Enough... Yet."

## HOW THIS LIMITING BELIEF
## MIGHT MANIFEST IN YOUR LIFE...

I think a lot of women really struggle with this limiting belief—that they are not smart enough or at least not smart enough yet. Countless clients and women I've spoken to share with me that they hardly ever speak up in meetings because they don't want to be seen as stupid. On Zoom meetings, if she is brave enough to share an idea, she looks immediately at the faces of all the attendees, especially executives or more "important" people on the call, trying to gauge the reactions. Are people nodding? Smiling? Looking bored or unimpressed? She's looking for immediate validation and feeling deflated if she isn't getting the validation she had hoped for. After the call, she beats herself up, telling herself she should have done it better, or should have just kept her mouth shut altogether.

I've felt like this for most of my life and now it's obvious that I haven't been alone. If you see yourself in one of these scenarios, chances are, you may also have a limiting belief about how smart and talented you are.

*Scenario 1:*

There's a job opening at your work, a promotion you'd totally love to go for, but you don't feel you are 100% qualified yet. You don't have all the skills they listed, so you don't even apply for it. News flash! Men will apply for positions that they are only 60% qualified for but women who are fully qualified (or even overqualified) often don't put themselves in the running because they believe they aren't the perfect candidate. They need to take another course first, or spend some more time mastering their skillset. You've got to stop allowing your imposter syndrome to win and instead, challenge her to a battle.

*Scenario 2:*

You've always dreamed of starting your own business. There have been so many fleeting moments where you thought of starting a podcast or a social media page that would motivate and empower a certain group of people. You've thought of starting your own clothing line, Etsy shop, or joining a network marketing team! But you keep not doing it because you don't feel qualified yet. "Who am I to start this online platform that encourages women to do XYZ? No one would listen to me, there's already so many influencers out there. Plus my family and friends would laugh at me if they found out." You've just disqualified yourself before ever giving yourself permission to ask the opposite questions. "Why not be the one to do this? Yes there are many women already doing it, but no one is exactly like me! What if my family and friends are inspired by me doing this?"

## ACTION STEPS:

1   **Reflection + Journaling Time:** Can you think of a memory in your childhood that told you that you're not smart enough? Can you think of a recent situation where you didn't feel smart enough? Have you experienced imposter syndrome or had the thought "who am I to do XYZ"? What does imposter syndrome stop you from trying or doing?

2   **Healing this limiting belief:** One of the best ways I know to overcome the limiting belief of "I'm not smart

enough" is by focusing on your innate strengths. I LOVE the Gallup Strengthsfinder Personality Assessment for this reason. By taking this personality test, you will begin to start owning your God-given strengths. You will be given a list of your top five strengths along with loads of supporting information. Stop trying to fix every weakness, or to be like someone else who is different from you. Find out what you're great at and hone in on it. Also, check out this fun fact: Gallup shares that the chances of having the exact same top five talent themes in the exact order as someone else is one in 33.39 million. Wild. We seriously are snowflakes, you guys.

**External Resources:** Google "What is imposter syndrome and how can you combat it? By Elizabeth Cox" for a great video on imposter syndrome. It's only four minutes, but wow is it helpful.

LIMITING BELIEF:
"I'm Not Smart Enough... Yet."

THE TRUTH:
I am smart and I bring numerous strengths to the table. My voice matters. My ideas and perspectives are valuable. I release the need to be perfect. I trust myself to figure it out on the fly. I'm committed to taking action before I feel ready. I believe in myself.

# *Chapter 9*

# LIMITING BELIEF: "VULNERABILITY IS WEAK."

I remember the first time I really let someone into my mess. It was the scariest thing ever. As you already know from all the previous chapters, I loved pretending like I had it all together and that life was perfect.

I was also fake vulnerable at that time, which seemed to make people like me more. I would pretend like I was an open book to people and I'd let them in really quickly. But I had this rule with myself: I can show 95% of myself to every person I meet, but there's 5% of me that I will NEVER share with ANYONE. And I felt really great about that rule because the 95% vulnerability seemed super vulnerable to everyone else and people felt really close to me. But I knew the truth. They didn't really know me. No one would ever be allowed into that 5%. The controlled vulnerability was my security blanket, my way to win people over but never get hurt. I felt untouchable.

At the end of my senior year of college, my boyfriend of six years, Craig, and I had been fighting more and more for a few months. We were in a couples bible study through my church (I basically forced him to go with me) and it was led by this cool couple—Heather and Kevin. I really appreciated their authenticity and how they kept the conversation real, talking about both the challenges of dating and marriage as well as the parts that are inexplicably beautiful.

On one particular day, Craig and I had gotten into a really, really big fight. I called Heather and Kevin and asked if I could come over after their kids went to bed so we could talk about it. I think I was hoping for some strategies or tools or, I don't know exactly what I was hoping for. I had no idea what a life-changing night it would ultimately become.

I was sitting on their couch, ugly crying, which I never ever did in front of anyone. And I'm not sure how it came up, but it did. I told them my deepest secret:

"I know this is super weird and crazy, but I think I'm supposed to die in a car accident in my twenties, and I'm 22, so I'm not sure when it's happening but I really feel like it might be coming soon."

Kevin stared at me with a strange look in his eye, one I wasn't expecting. He said, "Do you picture everyone coming to your funeral, and all the nice things they will say about you?"

"Oh my gosh. Yes…" I responded, so confused about how he knew!

"Do you picture how packed it is, and everyone is crying and wishing they had been better to you?"

Wow! I was floored. I nodded with wide eyes and disbelief, so he continued.

"I used to have those thoughts too."

I couldn't believe it. For the first time in my life I thought I wasn't crazy for thinking these horrible thoughts. Someone else also had them. Someone who was living a very happy, healthy, fulfilled life, nonetheless.

"Those thoughts are lies from Satan. He uses those dark thoughts to keep you paralyzed from ever truly living out your life's purpose. In fact, the individuals that God has really, really big plans for, Satan attacks even harder because he 100% does not want that individual to make the impact they're called to have."

All of a sudden, everything made so much sense. Everything Kevin was saying was clicking perfectly into my story. I had always felt like I wanted to do something big and impactful, but every time I would start to think about what that big thing might be, or what the impact would look like, I would think, *No, you can't. You're not good enough, and plus, you're probably going to die young so why even get started?* And I would give up immediately, disqualifying myself before even starting.

I wonder how many of us are disqualifying ourselves from doing something audacious before we even try.

Maybe your excuse has nothing to do with death. Maybe your excuse is that there's not enough time in the day to do that. Or that you would never be able to do it because you're not far enough along, so you'll wait until later to do it, once you have more qualifications and every duck is in a perfectly-aligned row.

As Kevin was saying all of this, and Heather was nodding in agreement, things were starting to make perfect sense. It may sound so obvious to you reading my story that of course I wasn't supposed to die in a car accident in my early twenties. But for me, that night and that conversation changed everything.

Kevin and Heather prayed over me in a way I had never been prayed over. They were actually calling these dark spirits of death out of me. At the time, the prayers were kinda freaking me out if I'm honest. I was crying a bunch, but also like, *What the heck is going on with these crazy prayers?* I now know this is called "deliverance"—which is basically when you have dark spirits living inside of you from your past that are holding on and impacting you. Spirit of Death. Spirit of Fear. Spirit of Unworthiness. They called those out of me in Jesus's name.

Now, if you're not a Christian (and even if you are a Christian) you might be reading this right now and getting *very* weirded out. Maybe you think what I believe is extremely strange and you disagree so strongly that this topic is rubbing you wrong.

You might even be tempted to put this book down, but bear with me for a second.

**I thought about deleting this part of the story during my book editing phase because I didn't want to freak anyone out.** The people-pleasing part of me thought about watering it down to make my readers more comfortable. But then I realized that I get to practice what I preach by being bold and sharing this authentically from my perspective. Removing parts of my story to make it more palatable for those who disagree with my point of view would take away from the 5% of vulnerability that I just told you that I'm leaning into. I'm committed to 100% vulnerability. I want to tell you the whole truth of how my life really changed that night.

For the longest time I thought my life changed that night because I showed vulnerability and shared it with two trusted individuals who honored and respected me, and called me to a higher place of truth. For the longest time I thought the shift that night happened because of Kevin saying, "I've walked the hard walk that you've walked." And for the first time I didn't feel so alone or crazy about my dark thoughts. And while I still think those two things were powerful and extremely helpful, I now believe something shifted in me on a spiritual level. My life changed like crazy after that night. All of a sudden I believed I was allowed to live my entire life, and to live my life to the absolute fullest.

There's a quote I saw on Instagram recently that said, "If you could believe in Santa Claus for ten years then you can believe in yourself for like five minutes." And I love that. I created a similar quote that I think is also true: "If you could believe in ghosts for ten years, then you can believe there's a spiritual world that has light spirits and dark spirits for like five minutes." I know some of you still believe in ghosts and are saging your house to cleanse said ghosts out.

So for five minutes, if you WERE to believe in light spirits and dark spirits, also known as angels and demons, then it wouldn't be that hard to believe that some of them might try to live inside of us—our body as their home.

I truly believe that the Spirit of Death was living inside me and left my body that night. All of a sudden I was acutely aware of all the lies I had been believing for so many years, the thoughts I had pushed further and further down inside of myself. And for the first time in my life, I truly believed that my life had a purpose. I didn't know what exactly that purpose was but that was okay. It was a shift that happened deep in my bones. A shift in my belief system.

Every so often, I'll feel that spirit or limiting belief try to make its way back into me. When I'm feeling lonely, hopeless, mad at the world. In those moments, in my feels, I can hear the taunting whisper, *Life would be easier if you were just dead.* Immediately I know that is not my voice and it's certainly not God's voice. And just like the t-shirt I saw recently, I respond with, "Not Today Satan." I do not allow that thought or that spirit to come back inside of me. He (or she) has no place inside of me.

I'm certainly no expert on this topic of deliverance, but if you are reading this and something weird is happening inside you where you're like *Whoa, this is hitting home in a very strange way*, and it's got you feeling emotional—please reach out to a deliverance specialist who can actually help you process this. See the action steps below for resources.

But maybe you're reading this and still just freaked out, weirded out, potentially judging me, and that's totally fine. I'm not offended. Even if you don't agree with any of this faith stuff I'm talking about, we can both simply agree to disagree while respecting each other's differences! So maybe for you, this really is just a conversation about dark limiting beliefs that you've created.

I often wonder what would have happened to my life if that night with Kevin and Heather never happened. There are no words to describe how wildly grateful I am for that night with this powerful couple. Because I chose to be vulnerable that night, it ended up saving me from my deepest, darkest reality.

## VULNERABILITY IS STRENGTH

When we think our vulnerability is a weakness, it causes us to shut others out when we're going through something hard because we think they would judge us for our mess. Or that maybe they don't have time for our sadness, and we don't want to burden them with our emotional heaviness. When we're going through a hard time, often the LAST thing we want to do is share what's going on out loud. Especially if you're the kind of person who is used to fixing other people's problems.

When we become brave enough to be vulnerable with the right people (safe people), we're able to experience a release.

Bringing your dark, negative thoughts out into the light releases the tight grip that shame has on you.

Here's another thought-provoking note on the limiting belief that vulnerability is weakness: We somehow think that we will be better liked because of our perfection. So we try to put up a front to make it seem like we've got this flawless life. But what's interesting is that the complete opposite is true. We connect most with people who are vulnerable and talk openly about their imperfections. We feel most disconnected from people who act like they're perfect. In fact, perfect people piss us off. I had a client tell me recently that she unfollows people on instagram that only post their highlight reels because it's so annoying. I don't know about you, but I'd rather be vulnerable and connect with people than appear to be perfect and disconnected.

So stop apologizing for your imperfections. Stop apologizing for having a bad day. Stop apologizing for crying happy tears or sad tears. Start embracing your flaws. Start showing your face without makeup in public and on social media. Start telling someone your day is sucking when they ask how you're doing instead of answering, "It's going well!" Start sharing your scary big goals with your family instead of keeping it a secret for fear of judgment. Vulnerability is going to look different for each one of us but I guarantee each one of us has room for improvement in this category of our lives.

A quick note for those personality types that are oversharers. (Or maybe you know someone who is an over-sharer and you're worried that by practicing vulnerability you're going to become like that person.) The root of oversharing is generally found in insecurity or in loneliness. The first antidote to this is to practice self-love. The second antidote to this is to ask questions. Vulnerability is practiced to build connection. If you share with immense vulnerability but never follow it with questions to the listener, it will become a one-sided relationship. Think of these conversations as ping pong. Once you've vulnerably shared your "ping," ask a great question to allow the other person to vulnerably share their "pong."

## HOW THIS LIMITING BELIEF MIGHT MANIFEST IN YOUR LIFE...

*Scenario 1:*

You're the person who is constantly saying, "I'm fine!" You know what FINE stands for? Feelings Initially Not Expressed. If you find yourself saying, "I'm fine," on a regular basis then this is a huge red flag that you are lacking the ability to be vulnerable. Often this is the same person that will judge other individuals who show too much vulnerability. If you're this person, then you think others are oversharing and wish they would "calm down." Or maybe deep down you are experiencing some jealousy because you wish you were brave enough to live your life like that. But because you've hardened yourself and tricked yourself into believing you're stronger because of it, you think those who talk too much about their emotions are weak.

*Scenario 2:*

You're always the hero or the helper. So you LOVE getting to support other people through hardship and solving their problems because that makes you feel really good about yourself. It pumps up your ego to be this "hero" all the time. But when you need help, you don't reach out. You love being the shoulder to cry on or the adviser, but you would never allow yourself to be the crier or receiver of the advice because it hurts your ego too much. Sometimes this can come down to a humility problem. In order to be vulnerable, you need to be humble.

## ACTION STEPS:

1 **Reflection + Journaling Time:** What is your definition of vulnerability? Who are you the most vulnerable with, and who are you the least vulnerable with? On a scale of one to ten, how would you rate yourself in vulnerability across the board? (With one being, "I suck at vulnerability and really need growth in this area," and ten being, "I'm extremely vulnerable and don't see a need for growth in this area.") What is one way you'd like to be more vulnerable? Who is one person you'd like to be more vulnerable with? Why do you think vulnerability is important?

2 **Healing this limiting belief:** Practice vulnerability in real time. The next time someone asks you how you're doing, pause for a moment and think about how you're REALLY doing. Sometimes it's worth repeating the question back

like, "hmm that's a great question… How AM I doing?" It will buy you some time to think about the honest truth. Respond by sharing one or two emotions that you've been experiencing that day. "I'm doing well! I've been feeling really grateful and hopeful today. How are you?" Or, "I'm kinda having a hard day, I've honestly been feeling overwhelmed and frustrated. What about you?"

By taking the time to give a genuine answer, you are also encouraging the other person to respond with authenticity and thoughtfulness as well. It will also likely open a deeper conversation because then the person might ask, "Oh really? Tell me more about why you're feeling that way."

The second way to practice vulnerability in real time is to play the game I call, "Say the thing you least want to say." I started using this technique with my now-husband Frankie during our dating time because he would ask a question and I would be tempted to share a half-truth because the whole truth felt way too vulnerable. I was never lying, I was just withholding certain information or thoughts that I felt like he might not want to hear. But since that's what I did with all of my other boyfriends and none of those worked out, I decided to try something new. Right when my brain would say, "Don't you dare tell him that thing!" I would challenge myself to say the exact thing that scared me most to say. I think I was worried that if he knew the full truth about me, he would break up with me. But of course, the exact opposite was true. So the next time you're having a conversation with a loved one about your life, play the game, "Say the thing you least want to say." (Note: Do NOT apply this game to gossiping about others or putting your loved one down. This game is for YOU sharing YOUR thoughts about YOU.)

3  **External Resources:** Watch "The Power of Vulnerability" TEDTalk by Brené Brown, or her Netflix special.

For a podcast on breaking free from dark spirits and more on deliverance, find the "Break Free—Ps. Becky Heinrichs" video on the Awaken Church YouTube channel.

If you want to seek Deliverance support, find our more about virtual and in-person options here: https://awakenchurch.com/ministries/awaken-recovery/

## LIMITING BELIEF:
### "Vulnerability is weak."

### THE TRUTH:
Vulnerability is strength. I am proud if myself for having the courage to share my authentic feelings even when it feels scary. Being vulnerable and asking for help is stronger than pretending everything is okay when it's not. I am loveable even with my imperfections and even when I'm struggling. My needs matter.

*Part Three*

# YOUR PRACTICAL
# NEXT STEPS

*Chapter 10*

# EXPANDING MY VISION

In my senior year of college, my friends started getting engaged and people would say, "Janelle, you're next!" I thought, No, I'm definitely not next. I don't want to be next because I'm not really happy with who I am and I'm not all that happy in my relationship either.

I remember driving home one day and sitting in my car at a red light. I was thinking about the kind of person that I'd want to marry—what his life looked like, what his character was like—and it hit me like a ton of bricks. The man with the character I would want to marry wouldn't want to marry *me. Ouch. That hurt.* My dream man is not going to fall in love with someone who is getting wasted on the weekends and is letting people think she's sleeping around. My future man is a gentleman who is on fire for his life and his faith, who is working out, going to bed early and waking up early. He certainly wasn't going to be attracted to someone who was living their life like me. I realized it was time for me to level up.

This brief yet insightful moment, combined with that influential night at Kevin and Heather's, began a transformation of how I saw myself and my life. It was the most insane, liberating feeling in the world—shifting from the belief that my life was destined for death to being like, "OMG I CAN DO ANYTHING I PUT MY MIND TO!!!!!! MY LIFE MATTERS! I MATTER!!" For the first time in my life, I gave myself permission to live my absolute best life.

What's weird is that as free as I felt, there was also a deeper subconscious shift. Seeds were being planted and I didn't realize how significant those seeds were until a few years later when I looked back at that time and was able to pinpoint the shift.

If you've been to any of my speaking engagements, you've heard me say this numerous times: *Your beliefs lead to your thoughts, your thoughts lead to your actions, and your actions lead to your results.* (Plus, it's the third time I'm mentioning it in this book!)

Even though I didn't know it at the time, my belief around my self-worth shifted that night on a subconscious level. And therefore, my results started to change.

My first result?

Within a month or so of that conversation, I broke up with Craig for the last and final time. He was a really great guy, but for some reason when I pictured myself living my best life, he was not in the picture. Not because he was a bad person, but because we had very different interests and wanted really different things for our life.

It happened in June of 2014, one month after my college graduation from Colorado State University. My indecision about our relationship had been so foggy and rollarcoastery for so many months (maybe even years if I'm honest with myself) when suddenly, it felt crystal clear. I was on a walk with my best friend and roommate at the time, McKenna, and I was telling her about my decision to break up with him. (I'm sure she was happy to hear after my indecisive blabbing away for the past few months—one day being hot, the next day being cold, telling her how confused I was.)

Tip: When you're with the right person, you don't feel confused 50% of the time. You feel perfectly peaceful and happy to be with your person.

"So I'm trying to decide when the perfect timing will be to break up with him," I told McKenna, "Because we have that concert this weekend which we already bought tickets to. And then the next weekend is July fourth and we're going camping and boating with Morgan and Blake and all of their friends. Then the next weekend his family and I are going to Grandby for his family birthday celebration, and then the weekend after that we have plans too! So I'm thinking maybe I'll break up with him like, first week of August? That way I won't have to cancel any of our plans, you know?"

McKenna listened intently, like she always did. She is such an incredible listener. But she wasn't *just* an incredible listener, she was also fiery and honest and told it like it was—which is a quality I have to have in all of my best friends because I love to be challenged.

"Janelle. You can NOT go do all those fun things with him for the next six weeks and then break up with him right after. That's so unfair of you to do. How do you think that would make him feel? What if he asks when you decided to break up with him and you say "Oh I decided in late June so I've just been going through the motions for the last six weeks?" Then he's going to feel betrayed and those last weekends together will be tainted. You just gotta rip the band-aid off. If you're already 100% sure, then don't put him—or yourself!—through more misery!"

Ugh. I knew she was right, and that sucked to hear. It would be easier to just wait six weeks.

"Plus," she continued, "What if you spend the next six weeks together doing all these super fun cool summer things and then you end up getting confused again? And then in August when you were going to break up with him, you end up not doing it, and you spend another six to twelve months together, and then you're right back where you started a year from now! Do you really want to get confused again? You've been confused for so many months now. You finally have clarity. You want to break up with him right?"

"Yes. 100% I know he's not my person, he's a great person, but he's not my puzzle piece."

Finding my "puzzle piece" was something I would always come back to.

I'm not sure if I heard about it somewhere or if I made it up, but I had this relationship theory called the Puzzle Piece Theory.

You know when you're a little kid and you're putting together a puzzle and you really want to fit a certain piece into an open space of the puzzle, and you can totally tell it doesn't belong there but you're frustrated and impatient to finish? The piece looks SO SIMILAR to the one that's supposed to go there and on top of that, you can't find the one that actually goes there, so you try to shove that piece into the puzzle slot? And because it doesn't actually belong there, it kinda morphs, ruins, or breaks one or both of the cardboard puzzle pieces that you're forcing together? And then it kinda ruins the whole puzzle in the end because eventually you do end up finding the right piece and it's basically too late because you ruined that one puzzle piece in the beginning?

Anyone else ever attempted this? Or was I just a destructive, impatient child?

Anywho, when you overcome the challenge of finding two puzzle pieces that are meant to work together, even though it took you a long time to find the perfect match, it just slides so easily into place, and you don't have to force anything. And the picture in the end is perfect because all the puzzle pieces are in the right place.

That's what I dreamed of with my future husband. I pictured us just fitting together so nicely that there was no forcing it, no trying to convince myself that it was right and hoping for the best. I dreamed of feeling complete peace about the man I was giving my whole heart to.

And so, I mostly followed McKenna's advice. I broke up with him on the Monday after our July fourth camping trip. I remember I acted so weird that whole weekend that I'm pretty sure he wasn't even surprised when it came on Monday afternoon.

Breaking up with someone after six years of dating was one of the hardest things I had ever done in my life. Even though I felt like it was the right decision at the moment, it was still heart-wrenching. It would have been, in some ways, so much easier to just stay with him. Because it wasn't THAT bad, in fact it was pretty good!

> But I was on a mission to live my best life.
> And in order to live my absolute best life,
> I had to let go of good to get great.

And so I did it. I broke up with my boyfriend of six years.

Even though I was brokenhearted, I felt that crazy unexplainable peace. Wouldn't you know, that night the company that I had been trying to get a job at for a few weeks called me for my first interview! There was hope in the air. I felt this strange sense of freedom that I hadn't felt in a very, very long time. For the first time in basically six years I felt the freedom to do whatever I wanted to do. I felt ready to start making choices that would get me to the life I most desired.

## THE NEXT BIG SHIFT...

This shift happened about eighteen months after that conversation with Heather and Kevin. Like I said, everything didn't happen overnight! But here it was.

I believe it was February of 2016 and I was living in Fort Collins, Colorado and working at a tech company called Encompass. My roommate Melissa and I were being asked by our property management company if we were planning to re-sign our lease in August. Since it was a college town, they made us re-sign our leases six months in advance, which seemed crazy to me then and still seems crazy to me now. (Like who really knows what they're doing with their life in 6 months?! Ha! Not me.) But anyway, Melissa had started to date someone and they were talking about moving in together, and I was thinking, "Cool, so I can either re-sign the lease and find a new roomie, or I could not re-sign the lease and move somewhere totally different, like, maybe even out of this city. Or maybe even out of this state!"

Here's the thing. I had been talking about moving to live by the ocean for years. YEARS! Back in college I had very lightly looked into studying abroad in Australia or New Zealand, but of course, with my small, fixed mindset, quickly deemed it too expensive and unrealistic, so I didn't find a way to make it happen.

My brother Austin and I had talked for a year or two about moving to California together but he met a new girl, and they got serious, and she didn't seem like she was on board for the California idea.

My friend Andrea and I talked about moving to California together too, but nothing seemed to be coming together on that front.

For a moment, I was actually going to move to San Diego with some friends, Victoria and Whitney. Then three or four months before we were going to move, Victoria met a guy in Colorado (that ended up becoming her husband, yay!) so she stayed put. Whitney and I actually didn't like each other very much so we didn't want to be roommates without Victoria in the picture. (Though now we are legit friends so that was an ironic turn of events for the two of us, also yay!) Anyway, there was yet another option that fell through the cracks.

The honest truth is, I tried to convince everyone I knew to move to California with me because I wanted so badly to live there by the ocean. I knew I wanted to be in Southern California. That's where I saw myself living my best life.

**But for the longest time, I didn't think I could go alone.**

I was waiting for all the stars to align and for it to finally feel easy and magical and perfect. And none of the stars were ever perfectly aligning. Ever. Every star that was supposed to align kept falling out of place. But still, deep down, I believed that the beach life was calling me.

So I took a leap of faith and decided not to sign the lease to renew my apartment. It was honestly really scary. I decided to take a risk and see what happened, hoping I could muster up enough courage to move somewhere new when my lease ended in six months. Rentals in Fort Collins go like hotcakes because it's a college town and I lived less than a mile from the college, so I knew that by not re-signing the lease that I was walking away for good. I was making this internal commitment to myself to take action on moving to a new city by August first. The pressure was on.

I began my plans for moving to California. I like to think of myself as a semi-calculated risk taker. I'm not afraid to make a big change, but it usually takes a few months of processing because I don't want to be too impulsive. So I like to take time for deliberation, prayer, lots of journaling, research, and making pros and cons lists.

I remember I was so worried thinking, *Does God want me to move to San Diego? Or does He not?* And I never felt like I had a super clear answer to that question. But what I knew was that I kept feeling a pull to do it. I kept feeling it in my gut. I couldn't stop thinking about it. Every time I'd try to picture staying in Colorado long term I would get sad and feel disappointed in myself for not taking on a bigger risk. And for me, all of those feelings were the answer from God that I was looking for.

So I decided to go for it. I told myself, "*Okay. I'm going to move to California for one year. Just twelve months. And if I love it and the doors open, then I'll stay. If I hate it or doors keep slamming shut in my face, then I'll go back to Colorado. It's just one year of my life. Twelve months from now I can come back to my life here if I want to and basically everything will still be where I left it.*"

So on the first of August 2016, my parents and brothers helped me pack up my U-haul in Fort Collins, Colorado and they drove with me across the United States to help me move to San Diego, California. 08-01-2016. My forever Cali-aversary.

I was so proud of myself for taking the leap. I still am proud of myself. I did it without a friend, sibling, boyfriend, barely any money and not even a real job waiting for me (just one small part-time job that was a joke compared to the job I was leaving behind).

Because the belief around what's possible for my life completely shifted, my thoughts, actions and results started to change too.

Some of it happened overnight, and some of it happened over time.

## LET'S TALK ABOUT YOU.

Have you had your first big mindset shift? If not, it's time for you to have it.

What is the limiting belief you will no longer stand for, the lie you've been holding on to that you are choosing to release today?

And what's the truth you are choosing to believe?

And how will this mindset shift change your life? What parts of your life will be different, now that you fully believe the truth?

The night with Kevin and Heather was the first big mindset shift of many I had. I wish I could sit here and tell you that all of a sudden my life became perfect in every area, but I didn't overcome every limiting belief all at once.

There have been so many limiting beliefs that I have uncovered in the last six years:

- Marriage is hard. It's constant work and very little happiness, you just have to stick together and make it work over the years.

- You're not far enough along in life to be a public speaker. And, you can't impact people's lives because you're too imperfect and mess up so much—you have no place to help people in their struggles.

- It's not good to make too much money as a Christian because then you'll be distracted from your love of God. If you struggle with money then you'll be closer to God.

- Your husband is always going to make more money than you. It's not a woman's job to make a lot of money, it's her job to make a little bit of money and to spend her time managing their social life and the affairs of the home.

## A FEW TOOLS I LIVE BY...

As you evolve and grow as a human, and the more reflection you do and self awareness you gain, the more often limiting beliefs will begin to reveal themselves. You'll start to realize all the subliminal messages that you were taught from your family, your friends, your teachers, the kids at school, the media, your coworkers—and the list goes on.

People are constantly throwing their limiting beliefs on to you. And it's not easy to ignore these opinions, especially when they're coming from people you love and respect so much. It's quite challenging and confusing.

One of the word tools I love to use is ,"I receive that" or, "I don't receive that."

## RECEIVING COMPLIMENTS

When someone gives me a compliment, or affirms me in any way, instead of shrugging it off and being like, "Oh whatever, pshhh," I receive it by simply saying, "Thank you, I receive that." Think of their compliment like a birthday present. You wouldn't take the birthday present someone just handed to you and push it away, try to give it back or get rid of it, would you? Imagine how offended that person would feel! So, think of a compliment as a present. Receive the present with grace, and allow yourself to fully enjoy the present. It feels better for both parties!

## BLOCKING NEGATIVITY

On the flip side, if someone speaks something over your life that you don't want to receive, saying, "I don't receive that," is one of the most powerful ways to not allow their negative or rude feedback to enter your mindset. If your mom makes an offhand comment like, "Well you know, we come from a family of divorces so you can probably expect one too." You have authority to say, "Mom, I don't receive that. I will be in a lasting, joyful marriage. Please don't speak divorce over my future marriage."

Or if the voice in your head tries to tell you, "Dang, I'm always going to be fat." You can look yourself in the eyes and say, "I don't receive that. I am stepping into the healthiest version of myself today and my body is reflecting my healthy lifestyle."

It's SO insanely important for you to begin catching the limiting beliefs being spoken over your life by yourself and by others, and to be active in protecting your mind from receiving it. The verbal acknowledgement of receiving a compliment, or a verbal block from negativity will allow you to inform yourself what you're worthy of, and what you're not worthy of. Step into your power.

# Chapter 11

# YOUR ONE PRECIOUS LIFE

The truth is that each of us really does only get this one life to live.

I'm not trying to be morbid, but I do think it's worth doing some quick math about your life. Let's say you're thirty-two years old and you're planning to live a nice, long, healthy life and then pass away peacefully in your sleep when you're ninety-five years old. That means you have sixty-three more years left to live! Which is 22,995 more days. Which kind of sounds like a lot, but also puts things in perspective. The honest truth of it is that our days are limited and so I urge you to stop waiting around to do the thing you most want to do.

It's time to take responsibility for where you're at right now, and then take responsibility for the next steps that need to be taken. Now, they can't all be taken at the same time, so it's important to prioritize your timeline a bit. You can't control everything, but creating a game plan is a great way to take accountability.

The last six years of my life have been a time where I've started to take 100% ownership for the life I'm living and I no longer allow myself to be a victim of my circumstances.

## VICTIM MINDSET VS HERO MINDSET

A victim mindset belongs to a woman who believes that life is hard all the time. She's a victim in her story because she believes life is happening *to* her. She's never at fault. She blames the people around her and thinks they're the problem. People are always trying to screw her over and she's always getting the short end of the stick. The world is out to get her.

This kind of mindset can often go hand in hand with a fixed mindset. A woman with a fixed mindset sees life through this lens: if she's good at something, she'll keep doing it. But if she's bad at something, she gives up immediately… even if she needs to improve at that thing in order to reach her biggest dreams. She takes everything people say personally because she's subconsciously looking for ways to confirm that she isn't lovable, or awesome, or doesn't have anything special to offer the world.

When this woman fails, she beats herself up saying, *"I knew I was going to suck at that! I hate trying new things. Of course I screwed up, I always do."*

On the other hand, a woman with a growth mindset believes she's the hero of her story.

This woman loves a good challenge put in front of her because she trusts herself to overcome that challenge! She repeats in her head daily, *"Failure is an opportunity to grow so I will take leaps of faith that scare the living crap out of me because the worst thing that happens is I learn a valuable lesson!"*

She decides that she likes to try new things, she decides to have a positive attitude and she decides that she can get good at whatever the hell she wants to! This woman is open to constructive feedback because she's hungry to get better. This woman is powerful, fierce, and loving because she decides to be. She takes 100% responsibility for the life that she's living and makes the changes necessary to live her best life. She sees herself as Wonder Woman. She believes that she's the main character of this movie called life, and that the upbeat soundtrack plays to the beat of her footsteps.

Right now you might be thinking, *"Oh yeah, I'm for sure the Wonder Woman example, I definitely have a growth mindset!"* And maybe to an extent you do, but to be honest, you also might have a skewed perspective because we often want to see the best in ourselves. And maybe there are parts of your life that you do have a growth mindset, but is every area of your life in full growth mindset mode? I would challenge you to ask yourself if there are any areas of your life that you have found yourself occasionally having a fixed mindset on.

## TAKE 100% OWNERSHIP

For example, let's say you're not making as much money in your career as you like to, and you don't have the leadership title you thought you'd have by now. You find yourself almost subconsciously blaming your boss. Or maybe you're blaming the system or blaming some outside factors instead of looking yourself in the mirror and making the decision to put your big girl panties on and level up.

Or maybe you're on the opposite end of the spectrum and you're like, *"Oh my gosh, crap! I do have a fixed mindset. I suck! Dang it!"*

Or maybe you're somewhere in between.

Or maybe you have no idea where you're at!

I have a theory that everyone has a little bit of a fixed mindset inside of them on any given day, and that it takes constant awareness to choose a growth mindset. After almost six years of doing personal development work on myself, I still have moments in my day or in areas of my life where I find myself blaming others. Sometimes it's really hard to be honest with myself about the areas where I'm making excuses.

Having an honest conversation with yourself about the areas of your life that aren't going so well does NOT mean beating yourself up about it. In fact, it's the exact opposite. A growth mindset takes responsibility from a place of peaceful ownership. Take the emotion of frustration or anger out of it. Look at the situation with neutral eyes.

What is the thing you keep putting off because you're hoping the stars align perfectly? Are you waiting until someone does it with you because you're too afraid to do it alone? Are you waiting for permission from a certain friend or family member? What are you waiting for?

Maybe the stars will never align. Maybe it won't ever be easy. But will you have regrets on your deathbed for not making it happen anyway?

I do believe in discernment, and I'm a woman of prayer too. But if you've been praying for clarity on something for months or years now, maybe God is giving you full permission to try it out on your own. Or maybe you know what you're supposed to do but you're too afraid to do it.

## THE CONSTANT UNCOMFORT ZONE

Are you actually living your dream life? Seriously. You only get one life! Are you doing what makes you happy daily? Are you proud of the life you've created or at the very least proud of the life you're starting to create and the journey you're on?

If you're not living your dream life, wake up! Don't allow yourself to feel shame or sadness. Instead, take back your authority and choose a growth mindset. You're still alive. It's not too late to get started.

There's a Chinese proverb that says, "The best time to plant a tree was 20 years ago. The second best time is now." The same goes for you taking action on your dreams. Today is the perfect time to get started.

If someone else can do it, then so can you. There's nothing different between who you are and who the person is that has all the things you want. The only difference right now is likely your mindset. Or, if you are taking action on your dreams already, then the only difference is time. Your timing might turn out different than the timing you'd originally hoped for and that's totally normal. Keep taking action.

If you see someone that has the success that you want, the job title you want, the bank account you want, the peace and happiness that you want, the marriage you want, the family you want, heck, even the beautiful hair that you want, know that you can have any of those things. You can have anything you want.

But you won't ever get any of the things you want if you don't believe it's possible for you. And trust me when I say that I get it. It's hard to believe you can have something spectacular when you don't even see it yet. That's called faith and it's not easy at all.

I think about my decision to break up with Craig (and every other guy I broke up with in my dating journey), I was hoping that one day I would find this dream man who truly made my heart come alive. I had no idea if someone better even really existed or if it was just a figment of my imagination, but I had faith.

I think about my decision to move to San Diego, praying that I would love it and that it would be all I hoped it would be to live by the ocean in this gorgeous city. At the same time feeling like it might totally suck and I could hate it and come whimpering home with my tail between my legs, but I had faith.

And right now as I'm writing this book, I wonder if someone will actually read it when it's finished, maybe even hundreds or thousands of people might read it, and have their life changed in some way. I don't have a single guarantee of anyone wanting to read my work, but I have faith.

**So what is it for you? What is your risky action? What is your big dream?**

I hear a lot of women say they get sick of hearing this whole "follow your dreams" crap because they don't know their "one and only dream" so they don't even know where to start. And they feel frustrated that they don't know what their dream is, so it's not motivating to hear "follow your dreams." Instead it brings them anxiety.

Here's what I'll say to you: Make sure you're not pretending you don't know because the thing you actually want is so unrealistic that you're embarrassed.

A lot of times when I speak with women, they tell me they don't know what they'd like to do with their life, they don't know their dream. But then we start digging deeper and I find out they do actually know their dreams but they're discounting them as too big or crazy or they don't understand how to make it happen. Often they will pick something similar, but safer and less exciting instead.

**So, what are you pretending not to know?**

All of this reminds me of a recent conversation I had with a friend of mine. She told me that she wanted to stop being a teacher because she didn't love it, but she was kind of freaking out because she thought she'd be a teacher her whole life! Ever since she was a little girl her parents and teachers told her what a great teacher she would make, and she was always so excited to pursue this profession. But she tried it and she really didn't like it. So she decided she'd do one more year of teaching and then switch to something else but had no idea what to switch to. (And I'm SO proud of her for being willing to make this scary career change!)

She brainstormed for about six months and one idea that kept coming up was to create her own closet organization business. We were talking about this closet organization idea and she started to get cold feet. *"I'm sure it would be fun for a little while but gosh I don't know if that's really what I want to do long term. It's giving me anxiety to think about doing that every day, even if it is utilizing some of my strengths."*

The next day, I got an idea for her and thought I'd see what she thought. *"What if you were to become a blogger? I feel like you're constantly following bloggers and practicing the hair styling tutorials and you follow interior design bloggers and you love doing all their how-to videos! And you're so good at all of that! What if you made your own blog? And shared your own how-to videos?"*

I saw the way she lit up when I suggested this idea. Like she seriously lit up y'all.

But she shyly responded, *"You know I've thought of that before but there's just so many bloggers already and I don't think I'm qualified to tell people how to do stuff and plus how do bloggers even make money?"*

Bingo. We got to the root of the problem.

She wanted to be a blogger but because she didn't understand it, she disqualified herself and told herself it couldn't be done, especially with all the fierce competition. There aren't any closet organizers in her city, so she told herself that's what she should do. It was a practical decision. (Which is why it brought her anxiety to picture being stuck in that job too, because deep down she knew there was something better in store for her.)

And because of her practicality, she kept saying, *"I don't know what I want to do after teaching!!!"* But really what she was saying was: *"I have a big, audacious dream of what I could do after teaching but it's really scary so I'm avoiding saying it out loud!"*

**So let me ask you this again—what are you pretending not to know?**

I believe anyone can do ANYTHING they put their mind to, believe in and are willing to put their time and dedication into. (With very very small exceptions to this rule like maybe you can't be an astronaut if you don't have twenty-twenty vision, though maybe after LASIK you can?) So do I believe my friend can grow a six-figure blogging business if she wants to? 1,000,000% YES.

Maybe you have five different big dreams and don't know which one to pursue because all five of them sound really amazing! To that I would say pick one for now, and go all in on it. Trust that if you're meant to go down a different path later on, you can always switch down the road!

Sometimes our crazy, audacious dreams take time to build up to the revenue we most desire. For example, if you want to be an entrepreneur and start your own business, you might need to get a part-time job, like nannying or bartending, or a full-time job that's low stress and monotonous because it will support you in building up your first paid clients. If you work in corporate and want to change your current career trajectory, you might need to start from a much lower position and work your way back up. Your ego might be embarrassed to take this step back at first, but remember: Short-term sad face = long-term happy face. Short term sacrifice for long term gain.

Personal development guru Ed Mylett shared on his podcast about how broke he was while building his dreams. He was so poor that he and his wife had the water in their apartment shut off because they couldn't pay the bills, so they had to shower at a local YMCA, or something like that. But his net worth as of now is $450 million and he's changing millions of lives. Just like with stocks, the higher the risk, the higher the reward.

Let's pause to create the space for you to have a brainstorming session to begin freely exploring ideas of what you're wanting most out of life. I'm going to help you make three different categorized lists that will allow you to get creative about the career, impact, adventure and happiness that you truly desire.

## A FUN YET POWERFUL LITTLE JOURNALING SESH:

**List # 1:** If you're struggling to figure out your dream job, make a list of every job or career idea, job title, or job description you've ever considered, no matter how wild the idea is.

If you absolutely love your job and are elated to be on the career trajectory you're already on, then skip List # 1 and continue on to List # 2.

**List # 2 :** Purpose/Impact

Make a list of everything in the world that's ever broken your heart or frustrated you, and groups of people you'd like to help (hint: look at the painful parts of your life story that you've overcome or have made progress on).

Examples:

- Helping young girls get saved from sex trafficking
- Helping homeless people in my city have food to eat

- Helping women in my tech company feel supported and empowered
- Helping a diversity and inclusion non-profit to empower people of color and other under-represented groups
- Helping newly single mothers get the support they need during their difficult transition

Let it flow. See if you can list ten different ideas.

**List # 3** - Adventure/Happiness

Make a list of things that sound fun or cool or exciting to you that you wish you did more of, or could try out. It can be super random. Come up with a list of ten things. Big and small ideas of things that would make you very happy:

Examples:

- Go on a hot air balloon ride
- Go to a farmers market weekly
- Freshen up the interior design in my house
- Find a local meet up in my city to make new friends
- Be a guest on a podcast
- Make $300,000 yearly
- Go boating four times a year
- Buy a second home in Florida to Airbnb half the year, and live in half the year

- Go on a twenty minute walk in the middle of every work day
- Get on a dating app and go on a few dates

After you finish these three lists, circle one or two items from each list that you are most passionate about right now. You will then be looking at three to six of your highest priorities in this season of your life. It doesn't mean the others aren't equally as important, but it does mean that you can put those on the back burner for now because it's nearly impossible to make significant progress in ten directions all at once. Then, ask yourself which one of these matters most to me at this moment? Listen to your gut. Listen to your intuition. Choose *just one thing* you are going to do, try, or make progress toward in the next 24 hours. You might not know all the steps of how to get from where you are today to the goal you wrote down, but I'll bet you know one, two or three steps you could take immediately.

Now that you've done this fun and creative brain dumping sesh where you've written out all your dreams, goals, and ideas for impact, we will spend time in the next chapter diving into a deeper reflection of your current quality of life to evaluate where you're at today and gain clarity on where to focus your efforts in this season.

# Chapter 12

# LIFE ASSESSMENT

I used to bounce back and forth between thinking I was so awesome and better than everyone else to, Wow I suck and my life is the worst. This came from a place of always comparing. It's not to say that I never struggle with comparison anymore, but now I simply choose to compete with myself, empower myself, and become the best version of myself.

It's time for some real talk. No one likes to admit out loud that they have moments when their ego is HUGE, but let me tell you something. I've spoken to women about their thoughts as my full-time job for the last five years, so I know a lot of you have thought (or currently think) like this.

Sometimes our egos get inflated and we have this smug feeling. It's totally happened to me before! I've had moments when I've boosted my ego by deciding that I'm better than another woman. I've thought I'm prettier than her, more successful than her or whatever.

Then, later that day I meet a woman who is crushing it in life—she for sure makes more money than me and is more successful, and her body is better than mine, and her skin is perfect and glowing, etc. and all of a sudden I'm like, *"Wow I suck, my life isn't nearly as amazing as hers, she's really got everything together. I'm so far behind and I probably will never get to her level."* My ego bubble gets popped. I feel as small as an ant, and depressed about my life.

Both scenarios are unhealthy. Both scenarios are looking at other women to validate (or invalidate) who I am and how great my life is. Both are insecure ways of being.

So how did I let go of this way of thinking and being?

**The first step was simply seeing my own value as a constant.** For me, the revelation that each human life is precious and purpose-filled on earth, including my own, changed everything. I am a unique snowflake and I get to appreciate how one of a kind I am, first and foremost. Author Mel Robbins stated in her TEDxSF Talk, "How to stop screwing yourself over," that the odds of being born at the moment in time you were born, to the parents you were born to, with the DNA structure that you have, is one in four hundred trillion! Those are crazy odds, right?!

## IT'S SELF-REFLECTION TIME!

Let's take a moment to review where you're at in life. It's important to get an understanding of where you are right now so you can have clarity on where you want to go. This will be a valuable exercise for you to think about the areas of your life where you specifically want to make progress by measuring your current reality.

Take a moment to assess each area of your life:

Please rate yourself from 0 –10 on each of these categories (zero is I'm not currently happy in this area, and ten is I'm fully fulfilled and happy in this area). Then explain WHY you chose the number you did.

1. Faith/Spirituality (whatever that means to you!)
2. Mental/Emotional/Relationship with yourself
3. Romantic Relationship
4. Relationship with your Family, Kids
5. Relationship with your Friends
6. Career
7. Impact/Life Purpose
8. Finances (debt, savings, investments)
9. Location/Environment
10. Health & Fitness

Ask yourself which one or two of the above areas did you score yourself low on that you MOST WISH you were playing big in?

In those two areas, what would a ten out of ten look like? What's your biggest & best vision for those two areas of your life?

Lastly, ask yourself which one or two areas might need a little less focus in order to create space for the two that need more attention?

And then what if, instead of being mad at yourself for not already being a ten in these areas, you choose to give yourself grace and kindness and encouragement and take 100% responsibility for the changes that need to be made.

Repeat after me: "I am 100% responsible for living the life I want to live."

Come back to this life assessment every couple of years to continue to measure where you're at. It's so easy to get caught up in the day-to-day that we forget to zoom out and inspect how our life is truly going from a 30,000 foot view. What you focus on you create more of. Focus on looking at the larger picture of your life, instead of getting bombarded with the details.

*Chapter 13*

# TOOLS I USE DAILY

This entire book we've been talking about limiting beliefs and it might seem like I'm beating a dead horse. That's because I'm truly so passionate about you becoming aware of the lies you speak over yourself daily, many of which you have been confirming from such a young age.

The tools I use are not a "one-and-done" exercise. They are something I would encourage you to have awareness of daily and to actually journal about every couple of months— especially any time you're about to do something that is really uncomfortable. Like for me, writing this book was scary for me. So prior to starting, I wrote out all my limiting beliefs around what could go wrong, and then I wrote out all the truths. Any time I take on a new challenge, limiting beliefs attack me like crazy. They say for every new level there's a new devil, and I really believe that.

## TOOL #1
## MY FIVE STEP LIMITING BELIEF PROCESS

**Step 1.** Become aware of the limiting beliefs that are floating around in your mind, even subconscious ones that you pretend aren't there. Sometimes that means sitting in silence or thinking about doing something that you're really afraid of like public speaking (or whatever it is for you)!

**Step 2.** Write them down on a piece of paper with space in between to write the truth. Allow yourself to face them, even though it feels scary to acknowledge them. The reason writing it down is so important is because it gets those thoughts out of your head, out of your mental/emotional world, and out into the physical world. Once it's in the physical world, you're able to digest it properly. When it's just floating around in your mind, it feels illusive and intangible. Writing it down makes it tangible, which is scarier at first, but then becomes liberating because you are truly facing the lie for the first time.

**Step 3.** Write down the truth—which is usually the exact opposite of the lie. Just because you write it down doesn't mean it will instantly feel true. Likely it won't feel like the truth right away, but the more you focus on the truth, the more it will begin to feel like the truth. It takes time. Trust the process.

**Step 4.** Tell a trusted friend. There's nothing more powerful than bringing your dark thoughts out into the light so they don't hold power over you any longer. I encourage you to share this with someone you trust—someone who isn't going to make you feel bad or silly for being vulnerable. Be sure to use the words like this—"A limiting belief I'm struggling with is…" and allow yourself to process the limiting belief, how it feels, and all the limiting beliefs that go along with it. And then say with authority and confidence, "Even though that limiting belief is there, I know that the truth is that… "

**Step 5.** Create personalized mantras. Take your truths from the journaling exercise and be sure they are written in sentence form. For example, if your limiting belief is that you think that everyone thinks you're dumb and are not capable of getting stuff done, then your truth is, "I am smart and I'm capable of completing anything I put my mind to,"—and that becomes your new mantra. In fact, it becomes a declaration over your life. You are DECLARING that this is your truth, period, end of story. I want you to look at yourself in the mirror every day and declare your truth mantra out loud with authority, power, and belief!

## TOOL #2
## IDEAL DAY WORKSHEET

Give yourself permission to dream big on this exercise. We often focus on everything we don't want but we forget to focus on what we do want. It's time to gain clarity on what your dream life actually looks like. I've added a worksheet to the back of this book that guides you through the process of imagining your dreams with a crystal clear vision.

## TOOL #3
## WHAT YOU LISTEN TO YOU BECOME

It's important to listen to personal development content on a regular basis, especially if you're struggling with negative thoughts. You've got to constantly put this inspiring content into your mind because our brains can easily fall into thoughts of victimhood. You won't feel like listening to this stuff when you're in a bad mood, the positivity will probably frustrate you at first. But you must choose to listen to it anyway until your mood changes. (See the four steps to getting out of a funky mood from chapter six.)

## TOOL #4
## ESTABLISH A POSITIVE MORNING ROUTINE

You've got to stop scrolling on Instagram and checking your email first thing in the morning. I beg you to stop. It will change your life to wake up the way people have been waking up for thousands of years, without technology. I challenge you to stop looking at your phone for the first thirty minutes of every day. Instead, make time for mindfulness. Make your bed. Chug seventeen ounces of water. Write down three things you're grateful for—practice gratitude for all the amazing things you already have. Write out your top dreams every day as if they've already happened. "I'm happy & blessed that I made $250,000 in 2022," or "I'm happy and blessed that I'm married to the man of my dreams." Don't stop speaking your dreams into existence until the day that you have it. This morning routine will help you keep your eye on the prize.

**TOOLS I USE DAILY**

Maybe you meditate, pray, read the bible, or dance it out to your favorite song! Start work and look at screens only after you've taken care of your mindset first and foremost.

## TOOL #5
## GIVE YOURSELF GRACE ON THE JOURNEY

It's so easy to scroll social media or read books or watch documentaries of other people who have done all this cool, successful stuff and to start comparing yourself to those people, wishing your life could look like theirs. But you have to realize that those people had (and still have) ups and downs and days where they wanted to give up too. (Hell, I'm in the final editing stages of this book and I want to give up!) Following your dreams doesn't always look or feel glamorous.

Here's what it might look like to give yourself grace: Take a mental health day to go on an adventure, or have fun with a friend, or sleep all day, or let yourself cry out the frustration. You could take a break from getting uncomfortable and give yourself some time to chill. You could think of someone you are inspired by and think about how hard their journey has been to get to where they are, which will remind you that it's okay to have non-linear progress.

There's a delicate balance between grace and grit. Too much grace and too much, "I have plenty of time, I'll get to it one day!" isn't good because then you likely will never get to it. But too much grit can lead to a hustle culture, which can lead to beating yourself up every time you don't accomplish your

151

goal. Not to mention exhaustion. Trust yourself to find the balance between grace and grit.

## TOOL # 6
## START DOING BREATHWORK

You guys, if someone told me two years ago that I would be suggesting breathing as a tool to you, I would have thought you were crazy. I was like, "we all breathe every day or else we wouldn't be alive... duh!" But what I didn't realize is that I wasn't properly breathing every day, mostly on work days from stress and heavy workload. But once I started doing breathing exercises, I became more aware of my breath in fight-or-flight situations, and now I know how to focus on slowing down my breath in order to stay calm under pressure.

WebMD says that the benefits of breathwork are:

- Balanced blood pressure
- More time in deep sleep
- Reduction of PTSD and feelings of trauma
- Stronger respiratory function
- Better immune system
- Release of stress hormones from your body

My favorite resource for breathwork is going to Wim Hof Sponsored events in my area. If you don't have any in-person breathwork events nearby, you can YouTube Wim Hof breathwork and he will teach you how to do it. At first it seems crazy, but after you finish a breathing session, you'll feel like you're on drugs in the best way possible, because you're high on your own oxygen. I seriously recommend giving it a try!

Another favorite resource is called square breathing. This one is great because you can do it anywhere and you can lower your heart rate in just sixty seconds by doing four rounds of breathing.

## Square Breathing Technique

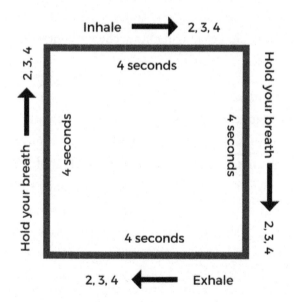

## TOOL # 7
## CUT THE COFFEE

Let me start by saying this: I love coffee. I love the taste of it. I love the smell of it. I love the ritual of it. And I've been drinking a cup or two a day for the last decade. If someone asked me if coffee has an impact on me, I would say no—other than making me a happy woman—it doesn't impact me. But what I didn't realize was that my heart rate went up when I drank it. And that there was this low level of anxiety (that I called excitement) that ran under the radar. There were a few times I tried to cut out coffee but was never successful because I would get a raging headache without it. Also known as withdrawal.

In the summer of 2021 I started to learn more about how coffee negatively impacts women's hormones and decided to challenge myself to thirty days without it. I wanted to prove to myself that I wasn't dependent on it. It took about three weeks to wean myself off it and yes it did kinda suck because I felt foggy and tired. But it's crazy because I sleep eight hours a night so I shouldn't have been foggy! It's because I was dependent.

Anyway, to make a long story long, by late August I was completely off it and once the fog cleared, I became the most peaceful I've ever been. Relaxed, calm, and clear-minded. My heart rate didn't spike anymore (other than natural adrenaline from workouts and work deadlines), my breathing naturally began to slow down, the pain in my body caused by stress went away, and my skin became more clear. Now, I drink chai, matcha or MUD\WTR in the morning because I love the ritual of drinking something yummy. I know not everyone reading this will resonate with this tool, but if you can't go a week or even a day without coffee, it might be worth weaning yourself off for a little while just to prove to yourself that you can and see for yourself if coffee really is providing you with what you think it is.

## TOOL # 8
## TAKE THESE FOUR SENTENCES
## OUT OF YOUR VOCABULARY

Here are four sentences that I have found make a person seem instantly less confident both at work and in their personal life as well. I posted this on TikTok and it went viral so I think it is worth including in my book as well.

1. **"Just wanted to follow up on this!"**

Get rid of the word "just" which is a word that is making you seem smaller. Instead say: "Following up on this email." Or, "Bumping this email to the top."

2. **"Oh sorry, let me just say this real quick."**

When you're trying to share your idea and you apologize before you even get it out, it makes people think your idea is going to suck so they're not going to listen. Instead what you can say is: "Great ideas everyone! One idea I have is _____."

### 3. "Oh no problem, I can take care of that!"

Stop volunteering to do everything. I know you're trying to be helpful but you're more valuable than always volunteering. Instead, Let someone else volunteer and you keep your mouth shut.

### 4. "Does that make sense?"

If you say this after you speak numerous times within one conversation, what you're telling people subconsciously is that you don't trust your voice. Instead, say what you need to say with confidence and if anyone has clarifying questions, let them ask. If you're teaching someone something and you're genuinely curious if they are getting it, then this sentence is supportive to sprinkle in. If you are presenting your ideas to an organization, leave this question out.

## TOOL # 9
## TURN OFF ALL NOTIFICATIONS ON YOUR PHONE

I was at a personal development conference almost five years ago where the main speaker encouraged everyone to take out their phone and turn off all notifications. Turn off email notifications. Turn off text notifications. Turn off all social media notifications. Everything. He explained that when you turn it all off, you get your life back. You become in control of your life and your time. You start living from a place of being proactive instead of reactive. You will still go and check texts, emails, and everything else. You'll just do it when you decide to, instead of when you get a notification that tells you to.

If you watch *The Social Dilemma* on Netflix then you'll understand why they REALLY want you to have notifications turned on from a psychological perspective. So I accepted that challenge then and there and haven't looked back. It was one of the best decisions of my life. Oh and I turned off all notifications on my Apple Watch too. Now, if I'm at coffee with a friend, I'm fully present, without screens lighting up or buzzing or ringing. I'll check my technology when I want to check my technology. I'm of the opinion that we are all on it too much already, I don't need notifications to get me on there more than I already am. So turning off notifications is a great way to implement more boundaries on your phone.

## TOOL # 10
## TAKE ONE DAY OFF SOCIAL MEDIA EACH WEEK

This one is pretty straight forward. Taking one day off social media weekly has greatly improved my mindset and happiness. I've done numerous social media fasts over the years. Sometimes for a few days, sometimes a week or so. One time I did three whole months, and that was while I was growing my business! I've shared this tool on social media numerous times and have had many people in my audience reach out and share that they started doing it too and it's one of their favorite habits. It's like a reset button for your mental health.

## TOOL # 11
## WORKING OUT (BIG SHOCKER)

The problem is that we often have this all-or-nothing mentality when it comes to working out and moving our body. Like, I need to either go to the gym for sixty minutes or not go at all. But the reality is that even if it's a twenty or thirty minute walk or a twenty or thirty minute at home HIIT workout, SOMETHING is always better than NOTHING. There are many days where I feel like I have way too much on my plate to make time for working out. But the reality is that there's too much to do to NOT workout. Will I get more done with eight hours of work and no workout or seven hours of work with a workout? (Thirty minute workout + shower and getting ready).

Trick question. The answer is seven hours with a workout because the exercise gives you a burst of energy that allows you to be more productive. Likely every reader knows this to be true, and no one is having their mind blown with new information right now. But in the heat of a moment of trying to be effective at work, we think that taking a break to workout or walk is the worst idea ever. So this is your reminder. Make time for your health. What's the point of working on your dream if you're not around to enjoy it twenty years from now?

## TOOL # 12
## WRITE THE EMAIL ONCE AND SEND IT

Do you ever struggle with rewriting an important email to an important person for a half hour or more because you're reading it and editing it over, and over, and over again? If you answered yes, you're not alone. This is unfortunately a sign of low confidence, at least low confidence in the work that you're doing at that moment. Your time is more valuable than this and you are more valuable than wasting your time in this way. Release the perfection. Write it one time. Read it one time and make any edits necessary. Then send it. Don't let yourself start to read it a second time, a third time, a fourth time—don't let yourself obsess over it being "just right."

Trust your voice and trust that it's good enough. You have bigger fish to fry. Who cares if you used too many exclamation points and who cares if you spelled one word wrong. Just be yourself and write that email freely. This will help you get your time back and to focus on more important things than perfect emails.

While a lot of this book talks about overcoming limiting beliefs and finally taking action on your biggest, most audacious dreams, this list of tools provides some of the smaller daily habits that make those dreams possible.

Let me ask you this: Would you rather have a single penny doubling every day for a month or would you rather have a million dollars today?

At first glance, the obvious choice is a million dollars today. But if you did the math, you'd find that a penny doubling every day for thirty days is $5,368,709.12. Wowza!!! Just imagine if it was a month with 31 days in it, that's over ten million dollars! I don't know about you but I'll wait thirty days to get the ten million instead of taking the one million today.

This story highlights the power of compound interest. Just like you shouldn't underestimate the power of the penny, don't underestimate the power of small habits. I encourage you to immediately implement at least one of the above habits even if it seems like it's not that big of a deal. And if you're feeling extra brave, pick the one that sounded the most uncomfortable. That might be your sign that it's the one you need in your life most.

# CONCLUSION

There's a statistic somewhere on the interwebs that says you only retain 20% of information from simply reading a book, but if you take action you will be able to retain 80% and if you teach someone else you will retain 90–100%. I know that we covered a lot of details in this book and that there are lots of action steps and tools you could implement immediately. If you're anything like me, you might want to implement ten things today but then one week from now you burn out on all of them.

My ask for you is this: Instead of burning out or having analysis paralysis, choose ONE action item from this book to implement immediately. Rome wasn't built in a day.

I also encourage you to re-read this book quarterly or yearly. I recently learned from a famous entrepreneur that instead of reading, let's say, fifty new books, he reads the same five books five to ten times each so that he really gets it. He chooses quality over quantity. And that's what I started implementing as well! Each time you read the book from cover to cover, or even if you simply pick it up and read a single chapter, you will get new fresh gold nuggets from it. More of it will permeate your conscious and subconscious mind.

**And if I could have you walk away from this book truly believing one thing, it would be believing at the core of who you are that your life matters.** You. Not someone else reading this book, not a cliche. I'm talking to YOU. YOU are more powerful than you realize. You weren't born by mistake. Your creator doesn't make mistakes. God has a specific purpose for your life, even if you don't know exactly what it is today.

It doesn't matter your age, the color of your skin, the size or shape of your body, or anything else, you DESERVE to feel confident in exactly who you are today. You DESERVE to see yourself as the gift that you are to this world. Please unashamedly OWN your strengths and step into your power!

Your limiting beliefs will try to tear you down and tell you that you aren't worthy of greatness. Your limiting beliefs will keep you small and have you making choices that are safe. Your limiting beliefs want you to live a mediocre life, running in circles on a hamster wheel. But you are a leader and world changer that's not going to stand for that BS.

Yes, we all have limiting beliefs and it's an ongoing journey of uncovering them in order to overcome their tight grip on our life.

We get to punch our limiting beliefs in the face daily and constantly and intentionally choose a new truth for ourselves.

Steve Jobs says you can't connect the dots looking forward, you can only connect them looking backwards.

So as I look back at my life, I realize that if I didn't overcome my limiting beliefs, I wouldn't be living the amazing, healthy, empowered life I am today. I would probably have settled for a less than average job, in an average marriage, surrounded by average people. Which would be okay, I suppose. But I wasn't born for average. And if you've read this far, then neither were you. You weren't born for average, okay, or even just good. **You were born for the extraordinary.**

I wrote this book for you because I KNOW beyond a shadow of doubt that if I could do it, then anyone can. I know it's possible for you to retrain your brain for success, to unlock dormant dreams inside, and to give yourself permission to break free from the lies. I know what's in store for your future as you continue choosing to believe the truth about your worth and you finally start taking action on your life!

You are no longer the woman asking yourself, "Who am I to do this really audacious and cool thing with my life? I'm just me."

You are now the woman who asks, "Why *not* me?"

And not only that, you are now the woman inspiring other women and men to take action on *their* life because they see you leading from the front like the boss that you are.

So I pass this baton on to you. Now it's your turn. **Get out there and flex your confidence muscle.**

# RESOURCES AND WORKSHEETS

## CONTINUALLY UPDATED CONFIDENCE RESOURCES

Scan here to discover powerful resources to build your confidence both personally & professionally.

Or, go to www.nextlevelconfident.com/bookresources.

## LIMITING BELIEFS AND TRUTHS

Do you remember at the beginning of this book when I gave you that long list of the most common limiting beliefs I hear? Well, I didn't want to leave you hanging on that, so I've provided a powerful truth mantra that combats each lie. Find the limiting beliefs from this list that you most resonate with and then write only the truths on a piece of paper or in a notepad on your phone. Say the truths out loud every day, with authority in your voice, preferably while looking in the mirror, as your daily affirmations. Feel welcome to make edits to the truth mantras to make them as empowering as possible for you personally.

———————

**Limiting Belief:** I'm not _____ enough. (I'm not good enough. I'm not outgoing enough.)

**The Truth:** I am enough exactly as I am today. While I am committed to constantly growing, I am also committed to seeing my innate worth that I was born with.

———————

**Limiting Belief:** Someone else would do it better. Someone else is already doing it. Or there's lots of people already doing it, the market is already saturated, what would I have to offer?

**The Truth:** There is an abundance of spots available. While there are lots of people already doing it, no one will do it the same way I will do it because no one is just like me. I trust myself to do this with my own unique spin on it. I trust myself to add immense value.

———————

**Limiting Belief:** I'm too busy! I can't start today but I'll start tomorrow. (Repeating this sentence daily for years on end.)

**The Truth:** While yes my schedule is very full, I am committed to prioritizing my calendar and making time for the things that truly matter. I will slow down long enough to reflect on my priorities, be willing to say no to things that are distractions, and say yes to the most important things.

––––––––––––––

**Limiting Belief:** I'm bad at confrontation and having hard conversations.

**The Truth:** I am committed to pressing into hard conversations because I know that staying quiet is doing a disservice to myself and others. I trust myself to be brave and say what needs to be said with clarity, honesty and respect.

––––––––––––––

**Limiting Belief:** I'm an outsider, I'm different from other people, people don't like me very much.

**The Truth:** I'm an insider. I belong. I am valuable and lovable exactly as I am. It's okay if I don't fit in everywhere I go. I release the need to people please. I am enough just as I am today.

––––––––––––––

**Limiting Belief:** People think I'm annoying. People think I'm too much.

**The Truth:** Likely no one thinks I'm annoying, people enjoy being around me because I have an awesome personality. If anyone does think I'm annoying, then they're not my people and I don't need to prove them differently.

---

**Limiting Belief:** I can't have both. I'll either be successful at work or successful at home, having both be super successful is impossible.

**The Truth:** I can have it all. Now this doesn't mean I can do it all, which means there will be boundaries and sacrifices made along the way both in my career and in my personal life, but I am allowed to be extremely successful in both work and home at the same time.

---

**Limiting Belief:** I have to work long hard hours to be financially successful.

**The Truth:** Working hard is something that society has taught me to keep me on a hamster wheel. Hard work and financial abundance are not linear. I will work diligently on the things that give me the best output with efficiency and effectiveness. Often less is more. 80% of my results come from 20% of my effort so I will focus on that 20%. I allow myself to easily attract financial abundance.

---

**Limiting Belief:** I have to do it perfectly. And if I don't, I beat myself up.

**The Truth:** I release the need to do it perfectly. Done is better than perfect. I'm proud of myself for completing the task with imperfection. I will continue to learn from my mistakes.

I will encourage myself after I complete the task no matter the outcome.

---

**Limiting Belief:** I'm not very smart. Everyone else is smarter than I am.

**The Truth:** I am smart and I was born smart. Everyone is smart in their own way. I have valuable ideas and thoughts that are worth sharing. I will focus on building myself up for my natural gifts and choose to be in encouraging environments where we affirm each other. Likely no one thinks I'm dumb, but if someone does, it's not my job to prove anything to them!

---

**Limiting Belief:** Life is so hard for me. Other people just have it so easy.

**The Truth:** While my circumstances might be more challenging than others I know, I will not be a victim to my circumstances. I am a hero. I can overcome anything. I have control over my mind and thoughts and will choose to see the best in things.

---

**Limiting Belief:** I'm not very pretty, I'm kind of the ugly duckling of my friends.

**The Truth:** I am beautiful inside and out. I release the need to compare my looks to others. I am committed to looking in the mirror and finding things to compliment about myself.

---

**Limiting Belief:** If I fail I should just give up, it must not be a good fit for me.

**The Truth:** Everything is figureoutable. Failures and short-term setbacks are learning lessons. I get to decide if I want to try again or not, the failure won't determine that for me. I am strong enough to try again, this time with new strategies!

---

**Limiting Belief:** I can't be a leader or impact people's lives because I'm so imperfect and I mess up so much.

**The Truth:** Yes, I am imperfect, but sharing my imperfections with vulnerability will help me be a leader & change lives in a big way. Fake perfection isn't as inspiring as being brave enough to show flaws and be human. I am committed to leading with love and vulnerability.

---

**Limiting Belief:** If I really say what's on my mind I'll hurt other people's feelings or make a fool out of myself so I'd rather say nothing at all.

**The Truth:** As Brené Brown says, clear is kind and unclear is unkind. By me saying what's on my mind and providing helpful feedback, I'm actually being kind. I am more than capable of saying what I need to say with love, confidence and respect.

_____

**Limiting Belief:** I'm just naturally a less confident person. Nothing will ever change that.

**The Truth:** I choose to have a growth mindset. I can get better and grow into anything I want. I am a confident leader and choose to step into that every single day.

_____

**Limiting Belief:** I'll be happy once _____. (Once I lose weight. Once I get the raise. Once I meet my significant other).

**The Truth:** I choose to be happy today! My life is amazing. So many people would love to trade places with me! I choose to enjoy the journey and find things to be grateful for throughout my day.

_____

**Limiting Belief:** Either I'm good at something or I'm not. That's just the way that it is. I was born that way.

**The Truth:** I have everything inside of me needed to figure it out as well as access to an abundance of resources to make it happen. I can evolve into whoever and whatever I want to evolve into. While I have amazing natural strengths, I will never use my weaknesses as an excuse to not accomplish my dreams.

## IDEAL DAY WORKSHEET

This is your ideal DREAM day so don't you dare hold back! Also, because this is your dream life, I *do not* want you to write about a vacation day where you have a full-time job at home that you've escaped for a week in Hawaii. I'm all for taking lavish vacations, but I want you to answer these questions as if it is a "normal work day" in your ideal dream life. A Tuesday or a Wednesday in your world. You can say that you only "work" one hour for all I care, because you have passive income from your ten AirBnB rentals so all you're doing is answering five emails and two phone calls. That's totally fine because that means you've created a life you're not dreaming of escaping from.

The idea here is that you can build a life that you love so much that you aren't trying to escape it by constantly thinking about your next vacation. You can be laying in a pool or by the ocean or hiking in the mountains, or in Paris or the Maldives on this dream day, of course!! But I want you to describe that as a part of your "normal life."

Dream BIGGER than you think you should! Some of your ideas here should feel a little scary, uncomfortable and maybe even a little crazy.

Write down each answer in as much lavish detail as possible—details are great!

**Let's pretend that it is five years from now and all your wildest dreams have come true...**

- What time do I wake up in the morning?

- How do I feel as I wake up?

- Am I alone when I get up or do I have a spouse next to me?

- Am I in a house, up in the mountains, in a hotel, on a cruise ship, in a bungalow on the beach?

- What does my home look like?

- What do I hear as I wake up?

- What do I smell?

- What do I do right after I wake up? What's my routine like?

- What kind of family do I have?

- Do I work? If so, doing what?

- Do I work outside the house or from home, or both?

- How many hours a week do I work?

- What kind of financial life do I have?

- Describe in detail how much money is in your savings account, checking account, investment accounts, real estate, etc. And how much you make yearly. Remember: dream BIG.

- What are my hobbies?

- What kind of spiritual life do I have?

- How do I pursue my growth and evolution?

- What's my romantic and social life like?

- What kind of friendships do I have?

- How do I participate in community activities?

- What are my vacations like? How often? Who do I go with?

- What is my biggest accomplishment up to this date?

- Who are the people I want to interact with on my ideal day?

- What impact do I have on the world on my ideal day?

- What are the five emotions I feel throughout my ideal day?

- And lastly, is there anything from this ideal day that you can begin implementing today?

# ACKNOWLEDGMENTS

I would like to acknowledge with incredible gratitude the people in my life who have formed me into the leader I am today and have supported me on the beautiful journey of writing this book. That gratitude begins with my mom and dad for loving me so well and being there for me no matter what. Thank you for teaching me what it means to go against the grain and be brave, faithful, persistent, consistent, and vulnerable. I love you both so much. I'm also very thankful for my three wonderful brothers—Austin, Joel and Aaron—for not only giving me a great childhood, but also for being my friend and cheerleader today.

Next up are my real life mentors. Heather and Kevin Deese, if you read this book you already know that you changed the trajectory of my entire life. Thank you for speaking truth into me and always keeping it real even if it was hard to hear. Thank you to Kim O'Neil at Encompass for telling me I'm smart and teaching me that I have the power to figure out *anything* I put my mind to. Justin Flemming, thank you for buying my first website domain in 2017 and telling me I needed to start my personal brand. It never even occurred to me that I could do something like that. You sent me all those personal development books in the mail and it lit a fire in me. Jake Kauffman, my first ever mindset coach, you truly taught me the power of my mind. You planted seeds in me that are bearing fruit today. Thank you.

To my church in San Diego, Awaken, and our business mentorship, Pathfinders, thank you for teaching me that my success points people to God and it's a disservice to not shine bright. Lastly, thank you to Jesus, my number one North Star.

Then there are the mentors I follow from afar that don't even know the impact they have on my life. I remember when I stood on stage at a conference in LA called MITT, and announced that I would be speaking on stages all over the world as a blend of Tony Robbins and Brené Brown. Thank you Tony & Brené for your work. I'm thankful to each of these people that have inspired me for the last four to five years with all their books, podcasts, social media content and teaching: Rachel Hollis. Sara Blakely. Shawn Stevenson. Jen Sincero. Beyoncé. Jay Shetty. Dave Ramsey. Louise Hay. Dale Carnegie.

The team at Merack Publishing! Wow you kicked my butt into gear making this book happen! I legitimately don't know how an author could ever write a book without the support of a team like yours. Kelly, you really helped make my scattered thoughts come together in one cohesive book! The book cover design and social media posts and everything else have been amazing, from the bottom of my heart I am so grateful.

My closest friends who have believed in me, helped me make book edits, cover design choices, and cheered me through this book reminding me that I am a badass and I can indeed do this—Emma, Meg, Joe, McKenna, Teagan, Gen, Tam, Libby & Joel. Thank you for all the feedback and ideas that make this book what it is. And thank you to every woman in my community that has believed in me and loved on me. I'm such a lucky woman.

My coaching clients from the past, present and future that have entrusted me with their mindset, you helped me write this book more than anyone else. To the clients that have hired me to speak and host The Confidence Workshop for their organization, especially the ones in the beginning that hired me to speak without knowing if I could deliver value, thank you for believing in me.

And I saved the best for last. My husband, Frankie. The love of my life. My best friend in the entire world. You encourage me every single day to keep believing in my vision. You motivate me like crazy to never give up. Thank you for making me laugh until my stomach hurts and for holding me when I'm crying and having one of my "entrepreneurial breakdowns." Thank you for being my "coworker" and "business coach." Thank you for all the times you reminded me that I'm a world changer and that I'm going to be your sugar mama in no time at all. We're changing the world together, sweetness. I love you.

# About the Author

Janelle Lynnae is the Founder of Next Level Confident. She is a confidence coach, national speaker, thought leader and corporate workshop facilitator who teaches women how to shift negative thought patterns into empowered and confident ways of thinking and being. Her mission is to help every woman step into her power and see herself as the valuable badass she is.

Janelle lives in San Diego, CA and loves boxing, yoga, hanging out on the beach, reading personal development books and dancing with her husband in the kitchen. She's a woman of faith and dog mom to the adorable Deni. *Flex Your Confidence Muscle* is her debut book.

Website: nextlevelconfident.com
Instagram: @janelle_lynnae
TikTok: @janelle_lynnae
Linkedin: linkedin.com/in/janellelynnae

Made in the USA
Las Vegas, NV
15 March 2023

69125723R00114